MW00652501

LARKIN HOUSEWIVES' COOK BOOK

Good Things to Eat and How to Prepare Them

Five hundred and forty-eight recipes, of which four hundred and eighty are prize recipes selected from more than three thousand submitted by practical housekeepers in the Larkin Recipe Contests. Compiled especially for customers and friends of the Larkin Co. by the Larkin Kitchen.

Published by

Larkin Co.

Established, 1875 Pure Food Specialists

BUFFALO CHICAGO PEORIA

Local Branch: Philadelphia

415 F. 4529-15

TO the woman who takes pride in serving tasty and attractive dishes, who delights in placing on her table "Good Things to Eat," who wishes to have the means of "variety" ever at her command, this Cook Book will be a valuable and constant adviser.

It is interesting to note that it contains recipes from the North, South, East and West; the favorite recipes of practical and experienced housewives. No recipes were accepted from professional cooks but all from the homes of our many customers. We believe that this book will prove unique on account of the immense variety given.

Here will be found an answer to the question that is ever perplexing the housewife—what to serve for the coming meal. Here she will find most valuable suggestions that will enable her to prepare, in great variety and in a practical and economical way, delicious and appetizing dishes that will be a source of real satisfaction and extreme delight to those in her home who truly appreciate "Good Things to Eat."

"Now, good digestion wait on appetite,
And health on both!"

—SHAKESPEARE.

CONTENTS

How to Measure

Level Measurements Only Are Used In These Recipes

Flour, meal, powdered sugar and soda should be sifted before measuring. A cupful is measured level; do not shake down.

A cup, as used in these recipes, holds one-half pint (two gills) of liquid, or one-half pound of granulated sugar or butter. A tin or glass measuring-cup, divided into quarters and thirds, can be purchased at any house-furnishing store for ten cents.

To measure a level tablespoon or teaspoon, make smooth with a knife but do not pat down.

A half spoonful is measured by cutting in half lengthwise; a fourth spoonful by cutting a half spoonful crosswise a little nearer the handle of the spoon.

A "pinch" is as much as you can hold between the first finger and thumb.

A family scale is a great convenience, both for use in cooking and for weighing purchases.

Weights and Measures

16	tablespoons	equal	1 cup
3	teaspoons of liquid	"	1 tablespoon
4	tablespoons of liquid	"	½ gill or ¼ cup
2	gills	"	1 cup
2	cups	"	1 pint
4	" (2 pints)	"	1 quart
4	" of sifted flour	"	1 quart or 1 pound
2	" " butter	"	1 pound
½	cup " "	"	¼ pound or 4 ounces
2	cups " granulated sugar	"	1 pound
2½	" " powdered sugar	"	1 pound
1	pint " water or milk	"	1 pound
1	" " solid fat	"	1 pound
4	tablespoons of coffee	"	1 ounce
2	" " butter	"	1 ounce
2	" " sugar	"	1 ounce
4	" " flour	"	1 ounce

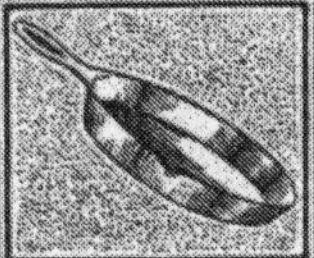

Rules for Testing and Using Fat for Frying

To Test Fat for Frying

1. Drop a piece of soft bread into the hot fat; if the bread browns in forty seconds, the temperature is right for any cooked mixture.

2. Use the same test for uncooked mixtures, allowing one minute for bread to brown. Fresh fat or oil should be used for batter and dough mixtures. It can then be used for fish, meat and croquettes, but should be frequently clarified.

To Clarify

Melt fat, add raw potato cut in small pieces, heat the fat gradually; when fat ceases to bubble and potatoes are well browned, strain through double cheese-cloth. The potato absorbs any odors or gases and collects some of the sediment. The remaining sediment will settle in the bottom of the pan. When you have only a small amount of fat to be clarified, add boiling water to the cold fat, stir vigorously and set aside to cool; the fat will float to the top and the sediment can be scraped from the bottom.

To Try Out Fat

Any odd pieces of fat may be tried out more easily in a double sauce-pan than by putting into the oven; it will then take less watching.

Sautéing

Sautéing is frying in a small quantity of fat. In many cases the word sauté might be used in this book but is not, as the word is not generally understood, so we have used the more common word "fry," which really means cooking in deep fat. All foods when fried should be drained on soft paper.

Fricasseeing

Fricasseeing is sautéing and cooking in a sauce.

To Egg and Crumb

Before frying, dip the mixture in bread-crumbs, then in the egg, then again in the crumbs. One tablespoon of cold water may be used with the egg to good advantage.

To prepare the crumbs put stale bread, thoroughly dried out, through the food-chopper, using the fine or coarse cutter according to the kind of crumbs required.

THE cheaper cuts of beef are best suited for the making of soup —the vein, neck, flank, cheek and shin. Though quite tough and sinewy they are full of nutriment and flavor.

Water cannot dissolve the fiber of the beef, so we therefore always remove the beef from the soup and make it over into meat dishes. The bones from roasts or poultry, or part of the steak from dinner, should all be put into a kettle, covered with cold water and simmered until the goodness is cooked out. Never boil soup-meat of any kind, for boiling hardens the meat without drawing out the goodness. Be quite sure to have a lid that closely fits the soup kettle or much of the goodness and flavor will pass off in the steam.

To Make Meat Soups

Wipe meat with clean cloth wrung out of cold water. Cut the lean meat in small pieces. By doing so a larger amount of surface is exposed to the water and the juices are readily drawn out. Always cover soup-meat with cold water and bring slowly to the boiling-point. If a portion of the meat is browned before adding water, the soup will have a richer flavor.

To Bind Soups

Cream soups and purees (purees are soups with the vegetables strained out or forced through a sieve) if allowed to stand, will separate, unless bound together. To bind a soup melt some butter, add an equal amount of flour and when mixed add a small quantity of the soup; then add to the remainder of the soup. In this way lumps will be avoided.

To Prevent Cream of Tomato Soup Curdling

Put soda with the tomato, allowing one-fourth teaspoon soda to two cups of tomatoes, then add to the thickened milk, stirring all the time. If you wish to keep the soup hot for a while, leave it in the separate sauce-pans and do not add the soda until ready to serve.

Croutons to Serve with Soup

These are made by cutting stale bread into thin slices. Remove the crust, spread with butter and bake until crisp and brown, or brown in the frying pan.

Beef Broth with Vegetables

Cook a beef bone with a little meat on it several hours in two quarts of water. When done, add one can of Larkin Tomatoes, three onions finely chopped, one pint chopped cabbage, one cup chopped potatoes, two tablespoons of Larkin Rice or Macaroni. Salt and pepper to season. Serve with oyster crackers. The vegetables are quickly chopped if put through Larkin Food-Chopper.

D. L. Nuzum, Watson, W. Va.

Mutton Broth

Put two pounds neck of mutton on to boil in two quarts of cold water. Add one turnip, one head of celery, one leek and one carrot, all cut fine. Cook for one hour. Then add two potatoes cut in dice and one-half cup of noodles or macaroni and one-fourth can Larkin Tomatoes.

Mrs. D. Leary, West Chester, Pa.

A Quick Soup

Take what is left of a roast that has a bone in it. Put it into a soup kettle, cover with cold water and simmer for one hour. Then add two tablespoons of Larkin Dehydro Soup Vegetables previously soaked in one-half cup of cold water for ten minutes. Add also four tablespoons of Larkin Rice and two potatoes cut in cubes. When nearly done, add one can of Larkin Tomato Soup, and salt and pepper to taste. Very good.

Mrs. Stewart, Paterson, N. J.

Pea Soup

Put one tablespoon of butter and two tablespoons of flour into a sauce-pan; cook until brown. Add one can of Larkin Peas and one and one-half cups of hot water. Season to taste with salt, pepper and a teaspoon of sugar. Add a little freshly-chopped parsley. Boil five minutes and serve.

Mrs. E. Varga, Chicago, Ill.

Lentil Soup

Wash one cup of dry lentils. Cover with cold water and soak over night. In the morning drain and add one quart of stock or water, one small bay leaf, one small onion, one teaspoon Larkin Salt and one-fourth of a teaspoon Larkin Pepper. Stew slowly for about two hours until done, press through a colander, then through a sieve. Blend two tablespoons butter and two of Larkin Flour, add to the soup, stir until boiling. Add one tablespoon of chopped parsley and serve.

Larkin Kitchen.

Bean Soup

Soak one pint of white beans over night. In the morning drain and cover with boiling water. When boiling add a pinch of Larkin Baking Soda, cook fifteen minutes. Drain again, add fresh water and simmer until tender. Pass through a colander, return to kettle, add Larkin Celery Salt and White Pepper to taste. Melt four tablespoons of Larkin Peanut Butter in hot water, add to the soup just before serving, also two tablespoons grated horseradish or one-half cup Larkin Chili Sauce. Serve hot.

MRS. L. W. PARSONS, LYONS, N. Y.

Marrow Bean Soup

When boiling beans for dinner save the water and use with left-over beans for soup. Put beans with the water through colander, allow one quart of milk to every pint of beans. Add salt, pepper and butter. This makes a delicious and also a nourishing soup.

MRS. H. L. MARKLE, LAWTON, MICH.

Pork and Bean Soup

Empty the contents of one can of Larkin Pork and Beans into a sauce-pan. Add one quart of boiling water, one small onion cut fine, one small bay leaf and a dash of cayenne pepper. Simmer one-half hour, then strain. Cook two tablespoons butter and two of flour, to a light brown. Gradually add a little of the soup until you have a smooth paste. Then add to the soup and cook five minutes. Serve at once with a few croutons in each plate.

MRS. E. LEIGHTON, BROOKLYN, N. Y.

Potato Soup

Peel one quart of potatoes and cut in dice, also one medium-sized onion. Put into kettle and cover with water. When tender add one cup of cream, pepper and salt and Larkin Celery Salt to season. Melt some butter in a frying-pan and brown one cup of bread-crumbs in this, to serve with the soup. Delicious.

MRS. W. R. TREON, TURBOTVILLE, PA.

Old-Fashioned Potato Soup

Take four good-sized potatoes, cut into dice; also two small onions finely chopped; add salt, pepper, celery salt and a small piece of bacon or a little butter. Cover with a quart of water. Cook slowly for one hour. Blend two tablespoons flour with one cup of milk. Add to the hot soup, stir until it comes to a boil. Cook for a few minutes. This is very good and will serve four people.

MRS. C. CROMAN, MARION, OHIO.

Cream of Potato Soup

Peel and cut into dice four large white potatoes and cover with boiling water. Cut up three medium-sized onions, fry to a golden brown in butter and add to the potatoes. When potatoes are quite soft, mash through a sieve using water and all. Add one pint of milk and two tablespoons each of butter and flour blended (the soup should be the consistency of good cream); add Larkin Salt, White Pepper and Celery Salt; also a few drops of onion extract and serve at once. MISS M. MAY, DARBY, PA.

Cream of Peanut Soup

Put one quart of milk into a double-boiler, then one small bay leaf, and one-half cup of Larkin Peanut Butter. Moisten three tablespoons Larkin Bread Flour in a little cold milk, add to hot milk and stir until thickened. Cook five minutes. Add one-half teaspoon each of Larkin Onion Extract and Celery Salt, and a little white pepper. Crisp Larkin Saltines in the oven to serve with this soup. MRS. H. WRENCH, GOODRICH, WIS.

Cream of Corn Soup

Put one can of Larkin Corn into a sauce-pan with one pint of hot water and a slice of onion. Simmer for twenty minutes, rub through a sieve and add one pint of milk. Blend together three tablespoons flour with three of butter. Add the hot soup gradually so it will not be lumpy. Stir until thickened. Add salt and pepper. Serve at once. LARKIN KITCHEN.

Tomato Soup

Cook together for twenty minutes, one can tomatoes, one pint water, twelve peppercorns, four cloves, two teaspoons sugar, small piece of bay leaf, and one small onion cut in slices. Strain and add one teaspoon salt, and one-eighth teaspoon soda. Melt two tablespoons butter, add three tablespoons flour, when thoroughly mixed add strained liquid, boil three minutes and it is ready to serve. If desired, one quart of milk may be scalded and added just before serving; you will then have Cream of Tomato Soup. MISS BESSIE RENFREW, LENOX, MASS.

Tomato Bouillon

Heat the contents of one can of Larkin Tomatoes to boiling point. Strain through a fine sieve. Add one-half teaspoon soda, one teaspoon salt, one pint of hot water and two Larkin Bouillon Cubes. Bring to a boil and it is ready to serve. It is exceedingly good and just the thing for a luncheon dish or when serving a heavy dinner. Serve with crackers.

MRS. B. RAYBURN TATE, MOBERLY, MO.

Tomato Soup with Macaroni

Put one cup of Larkin Short-Cut Macaroni to cook in one quart of boiling salted water. Cook about twenty minutes or until tender. Be careful it does not settle to bottom and scorch. When cooked add one-half can tomatoes and bring to a boil, add a pinch of soda, a generous piece of butter and one pint of rich milk. Season to taste with salt and pepper. Serve very hot.

FRANCES C. ARGETSINGER, VAN ETTEN, N. Y.

Vegetable Chowder

Put through Larkin Food-Chopper (using coarse cutter) one beet, two onions, two carrots, two parsnips, all medium-size; also four large potatoes, and one quart of fresh or canned tomatoes. Add two quarts boiling water, cook gently one hour, then add one tablespoon salt, one-half teaspoon pepper, two tablespoons granulated sugar, cook for thirty minutes longer and it is ready to serve. Sufficient for six people.

MRS. F. A. HOUGH, WORCESTER, MASS.

Corn Chowder

Chop fine, one-half cup or one-fourth pound of salt pork. Put into frying pan to try out. Then add to the fat, one thinly-sliced onion. Turn into a soup kettle. Add one can of Larkin Corn and three pints of milk. Thicken with diluted flour. Add pepper and salt. Place a Larkin Soda Cracker in each plate, pour the soup over it and serve.

MRS. H. F. SMITH, MORRISVILLE, VT.

Clam Chowder

Chop fine four potatoes, one large onion, four tomatoes, and one carrot and boil in two quarts of water; when nearly done add twenty-five clams, finely chopped, four tablespoons of butter and salt and pepper to taste.

MRS. HARRY C. SMITH, TRENTON, N. J.

Imperial Fish Chowder

Take two pounds of halibut or fresh codfish. Wash, remove the skin and bones, and chop coarsely. Also chop one pound of salt pork or Larkin Bacon, six medium-sized potatoes, two large onions, six fresh tomatoes or one-half can. Put all in a soup kettle, season with salt and pepper and pour over boiling water to almost cover. Simmer one hour or more over a moderate fire; do not stir. Rub together three tablespoons of butter with two of flour, heat a quart of milk and gradually add to the flour. Put a pinch of soda into the chowder, add the thickened milk, bring to a boil and serve at once.

MRS. W. H. BLISS, SHREWSBURY, MASS.

Salmon Chowder

Put one can of Larkin Red Salmon into a sauce-pan with one quart of milk. When hot add one teaspoon salt, a little white pepper and two tablespoons Larkin Cracker Meal. If Cream Soup is preferred strain through a sieve, put a teaspoon of whipped cream in center of each plate, and serve at once. Will serve five people.

MRS. S. D. COOK, LANSING, MICH.

Oyster Soup

Put one quart of oysters into colander and drain away liquid. Pick over to remove shells, pour over them one quart of cold water. Bring one quart of milk to scalding point, thicken with two tablespoons butter blended with two tablespoons flour. Then add oysters and liquor, one teaspoon salt and one-fourth teaspoon pepper; bring to a boil and serve at once. Do not allow soup to boil or the oysters will become hard.

LARKIN KITCHEN.

Cream of Clam Soup

One pint or twenty-five small clams, three cups of milk, one-half teaspoon Larkin Onion Extract, three tablespoons butter, three tablespoons flour, pepper and salt.

Pick over the clams and chop fine; put them with the liquor into a sauce-pan and bring to the boiling point. Melt the butter, add the flour, then the milk. Cook for a few minutes; add salt and pepper. Add milk to the clams, reheat and serve at once in individual soup plates, or in bouillon cups, with a spoon of whipped cream in each. Sprinkle a little fresh chopped parsley over the cream; add a dash of paprika, and a charming luncheon dish is the result.

MRS. A. B. GRACIA, NEW BEDFORD, MASS.

To Boil Fish

Wash the fish well in cold water, wipe carefully and rub with salt; wrap in a cloth, drop into a pan of boiling water; add a slice of onion, a bay leaf and one teaspoon of salt. Cover and simmer gently, allowing ten minutes to a pound, lift out carefully, drain, unfasten the cloth, garnish with parsley and lemon and serve with plain drawn butter or fish sauce.

LARKIN KITCHEN.

To Fry Fish

Wash and dry fish thoroughly. Dip in seasoned flour, then in egg and bread-crumbs. Fry in deep fat, drain on soft paper. Serve with sauce.

LARKIN KITCHEN.

Broiled Fish

Wash and split open a firm white fish and remove the bone. Spread with soft butter, dredge lightly with flour and season with pepper and salt. Place fish on a buttered pan or fish sheet and cook under the gas flame or over the open fire. The time required depends upon the thickness of the fish. With a Larkin Spatula remove from pan to hot platter. Garnish with slices of lemon and sprigs of parsley. Serve very hot.

LARKIN KITCHEN.

Planked Fish

Prepare fish as for broiling. Lay onto a buttered fish plank, skin side down. Bake in hot oven, of in broiling oven if a gas stove is used, for ten or fifteen minutes. If the fish is a thick one it is best to heat the plank before using and bake in a moderate oven. Surround fish with a thick border of well-seasoned mashed potatoes and bake until potatoes are slightly brown. Garnish with lemon and parsley. Serve hot.

LARKIN KITCHEN.

Baked Fish

Scale, clean, and wash the fish. Wipe it dry and fill with a stuffing made of one cup of mashed potatoes, one cup of stale bread-crumbs, seasoned with Larkin Pepper, Salt, chopped parsley and a tablespoon of butter. Sew up with a strong thread. Lay it in a baking-pan, put a tablespoon of butter or pork fat on top and dredge with flour. Add one-half cup of water. Put into Larkin Savory Roaster and bake in a moderate oven one hour or until the flesh readily separates from the bone. Serve hot.

MRS. D. LEARY, WEST CHESTER, PA.

Baked Shad with Tomatoes

Clean the fish. Brown one cup of bread-crumbs in butter, fill shad and sew up. Grease a baking-pan with butter. Take three pieces of Larkin Bacon, lay over shad, sprinkle with salt and pepper, baste with three tablespoons of Larkin Canned Tomatoes and three tablespoons of water. Bake one-half hour or longer, according to size.

MRS. C. ADAMS, HARRISBURG, PA.

Codfish Balls

Prepare one-half package or one generous cup of Larkin Pure Codfish as directed. Put into a sauce-pan with two raw potatoes cut into dice, cover with boiling water and bring slowly to boiling point. Cook for ten minutes, drain thoroughly and mash fine with wire potato-masher. Add one egg (unbeaten), pepper and salt if needed. Form into tiny balls with a spoon. Fry in hot fat. They are cooked when brown. Serve with egg sauce. This quantity will serve five people.

MRS. MARTIN BURNS, SCHENECTADY, N. Y.

Codfish Loaf

Soak one-half package of Larkin Pure Codfish in cold water three hours before using. Put into a sauce-pan with one and a half cups of diced raw potatoes. Simmer twenty minutes, drain off the water and beat light with a wire potato-masher. Melt three tablespoons of cooking fat or butter in a frying-pan. Add one and a half cups of onions (about four onions) sliced quite fine. Cook until brown. Add to the Codfish in the sauce-pan, mix together with two teaspoons of lemon juice, one teaspoon of Larkin Dry Mustard, a little pepper, salt if needed. Put into buttered Larkin Casserole and bake in hot oven twenty minutes. Serve with cream or egg sauce. These quantities will serve five people.

MRS. V. ZOOK, NEVADA, OHIO.

Creamed Codfish

Prepare one-half package of Larkin Pure Codfish as directed and cook for fifteen minutes. Make a cream sauce by melting two tablespoons butter, add two of flour and one cup of milk, season with salt and pepper. The beaten yolk of one egg may be used in the sauce if desired. Stir in the codfish and serve on toast. Sufficient to serve five people.

MRS. H. D. CLARK, CLARK'S SUMMIT, PA.

Codfish Fritters

Cut Larkin Pure Codfish into strips about the size of a finger. Freshen by soaking several hours in cold water. When needed, dry between the folds of a soft towel and dip each piece in a batter made by sifting together one cup of Larkin Flour, one teaspoon Larkin Baking Powder, one-half teaspoon salt and a few grains of pepper. Beat one egg quite light, add three-fourths of a cup of milk; gradually add to the flour, be sure to mix quite smooth. Fry a delicate brown in hot fat. Serve at once.

MRS. HUTTER, ROCHESTER, N. Y.

Baked Salmon Loaf

One can of Larkin Red Alaska Salmon, four tablespoons of bread-crumbs, four tablespoons butter, pepper and salt to taste. Add one egg slightly beaten. Mix thoroughly and bake in loaf with three slices of Larkin Bacon across the top. Serve with creamed onions.

MRS. E. A. ROSS, SPRINGFIELD, MASS.

Salmon Loaf

Mix together one can of Larkin Red Salmon, one cup of milk, one-half cup of cracker-crumbs, one egg slightly beaten, salt and pepper to taste. Bake in a bread-pan half an hour, turn out on a platter and pour around the loaf one pint of seasoned cream sauce to which you have added one cup of Larkin Green Peas. This loaf may be steamed one hour instead of baked if preferred.

MRS. J. KNOWLDEN, HINSDALE, N. Y.

Salmon Soufflé

Flake one can of Larkin Salmon, add one cup of bread- or cracker-crumbs soaked in two cups of milk. Season with salt, pepper, and the juice of one lemon. Then add the lightly-beaten yolks of three eggs. Fold in last the stiffly-beaten whites. Bake in a moderate oven twenty-five minutes. Serve with creamed potatoes.

MRS. EMMA G. BURROWS, AMHERST, MASS.

Salmon Croquettes

Mix one can of Larkin Salmon with one cup brown bread-crumbs, one cup of mashed potatoes, one-half teaspoon Larkin Salt, a little pepper, one egg slightly beaten and one tablespoon of melted butter. Form in croquettes and roll in bread-crumbs; then egg and crumbs again. Fry in hot fat.

DAISY E. LIGHT, MARTINSBURG, W. VA.

Creamed Oysters

Make a cream sauce by melting two tablespoons butter, add two tablespoons flour, stir in gradually one cup of milk; stir until boiling. Add one teaspoon salt and one-eighth teaspoon pepper. The beaten yolk of one egg may be added if liked. Scald twenty-five oysters in their own juice and add to cream sauce. Serve at once on buttered toast.

ANNA B. BOND, WOODENSBURG, MD.

Oysters au Gratin

Put two tablespoons butter into a sauce-pan. When melted add two tablespoons flour, and one cup of milk and stir until it thickens. When cooked, season with one-half teaspoon salt, a little pepper and one teaspoon of chopped parsley. Butter a baking dish. Put in a layer of sauce, then a layer of Larkin Cove Oysters. Sprinkle with salt and pepper, add more sauce and so on until all is used. Cover top with bread-crumbs or Larkin Cracker Meal. Dot thickly with butter and bake in a quick oven twenty-five minutes. Four tablespoons of grated cheese added to the sauce improves the flavor for some people.

MRS. J. A. HENRY, STRAWBERRY POINT, IOWA.

Fried Oysters

Put the oysters into a colander to drain; with the fingers place each one on a dry soft towel to absorb the moisture. Season with salt and pepper. Beat one egg; add one tablespoon cold water. Dip each oyster in the egg, then in stale bread- or cracker-crumbs or Larkin Cracker Meal. Fry in deep fat. Drain on soft paper. Serve on toast. Pass lemon with the oysters.

MRS. JNO. LATTIMORE, CLAYSVILLE, PA.

Little Pigs in Blankets

Choose large plump oysters and wrap a thin slice of Larkin Bacon around each one pinning it with a tooth pick. Put them into a heated frying-pan and cook until the bacon is crisp. Serve at once.

MRS. FANNY YOUNG, ALBION, MICH.

Shrimp in Ramekins

Melt four tablespoons of butter; add four tablespoons of Larkin Flour and when bubbling stir in one and one-half cups of milk. Season to taste with Larkin Salt and Pepper. Add two cans of Larkin Shrimp and one can of Larkin Canned Peas. Rinse both Shrimp and Peas with cold water, then drain. Fill either buttered ramekins or scallop sheels with the mixture or place in a Larkin Casserole. Sprinkle with buttered bread-crumbs and bake twenty minutes in a moderate oven. If prepared in chafing dish, serve on buttered toast.

MRS. J. R. ABERCROMBIE, ST. JOSEPH, MO.

Lobster Wiggle

Melt three tablespoons of butter, add three tablespoons of flour. When bubbling, gradually add two cups of milk or cream, stir until thickened. Add one cup of Larkin Canned Lobster broken into small pieces, one cup of Larkin Peas drained from liquor, one-half teaspoon Larkin Salt and one-eighth teaspoon pepper. Serve on buttered toast. Cold, cooked chicken or shrimps may be used in the same way. Shreds of green pepper may be used in place of peas.

MRS. E. A. BENHAM, SARATOGA SPRINGS, N. Y.

Clam Pie

Put one pint of clams or one can of Larkin Canned Clams through a food-chopper. With the liquor mix one tablespoon of Larkin Flour diluted with a little cold water, and add to clams. Season with salt and pepper. Line a deep pie-plate with pastry, pour in clams, and put on a top crust. Dot small pieces of butter over top crust and bake in a hot oven about twenty minutes.

MRS. CARL SOUTHWORTH, BRIDGEWATER, MASS.

To Pan Broil Steak

Have the steak a little more than one inch thick. Make an iron pan very hot, rub it quickly with suet, then put in the steak. Never put the fork into the lean meat, always in the fat. Just as soon as one side is seared, turn over; turn several times in cooking; add pepper and salt; serve on a hot dish at once.

LARKIN KITCHEN.

To Broil Steak

See that the fire is bright and clear, put the steak on the grid-iron, turn often and allow time according to the thickness of steak; dust with pepper and salt and serve very hot. Steak to be good should never stand after being cooked.

LARKIN KITCHEN.

To Broil with Gas

Light the gas in the oven at least five minutes before you wish to use it. Take out the rack or the meat will stick to the bars if very hot; leave in the lower pan. Put the steak on the rack as near the flame as you can without the flame touching. As soon as the steak is thoroughly seared, turn the meat over; be careful not to put the fork into the lean of the meat as that allows the juices to escape; turn once more and season liberally with salt and pepper. Drain off some of the fat in broiling pan and pour the remainder with the sediment over the steak. Serve at once.

LARKIN KITCHEN.

Pot Roast

Take four pounds of beef from the shoulder. Put half a cup of good drippings in an iron kettle, make hot and sear beef on each side; when well browned set back where it will cook slowly for two hours; after the first hour add salt and pepper, a piece of celery, carrot, onion and bay leaf if liked; if cooked slowly no water will be needed. Pour off some of the fat and make gravy as for roast beef.

LARKIN KITCHEN.

Roast Beef

Wipe meat with damp cloth, place in baking pan bone side down, dust lightly with pepper; if there is no fat with meat, cut up a piece of suet and place around beef. The oven must be very hot. After first twenty minutes, cool off oven a little, add salt. Allow fifteen minutes to the pound for cooking and, unless a covered roaster is used, baste every ten minutes. To make gravy, lift out beef, pour off fat, scrape together all brown sediment from around pan, allow two tablespoons flour to two of fat, mix well; then add hastily one pint of water or stock, boil up well, add salt and pepper, strain and serve.

LARKIN KITCHEN.

Swiss Steak

Have two pounds of round steak cut one inch thick. Melt two tablespoons of fat (suet will do) in a frying pan, season steak with salt and pepper, dredge with flour, brown quickly on both sides then put into a Larkin Casserole. Brown a scant half cup flour in fat left in pan, add three cups hot water, pour over the meat. Cook for two hours in a slow oven. If onion is liked, flavor with Larkin Onion Extract, or cook a raw onion in the fat before the meat is browned. The toughest meat will become tender and delicious, cooked in this way.

MRS. D. H. DAGER, LAFAYETTE HILL, PA.

Spanish Steak

Two pounds top round steak cut about two inches thick, leave on the fat. Brown in hot frying pan, then add three-fourths cup boiling water, cover and bake forty-five minutes in moderate oven. Sprinkle with salt and pepper; cover with layer sliced seasoned onions. Bake another hour. Then cover with layer of the solid meat of a can of Larkin Tomatoes. Bake again fifteen minutes. Sprinkle over top two tablespoons grated cheese; place in oven long enough for cheese to melt. There will be a delicious thick gravy and the steak will be very tender.

MRS. M. C. DURKIN, SHAMOKIN, PA.

Hamburg Steak with Tomato Sauce

Put one and a half pounds of round steak through the food-chopper, add one or two eggs, one cup of Larkin Cracker Meal or stale bread-crumbs, salt and pepper, one small onion finely chopped, water or milk to moisten; mix thoroughly. Form into small cakes. Cook slowly in a small quantity of hot fat. When steak is cooked, empty one can of Larkin Tomato Soup in frying pan, when boiling pour over steak and serve at once.

MRS. E. E. NOHL, CANTON, OHIO.

English Beef Steak Pudding

Sift three cups of Larkin Flour with two teaspoons of Larkin Baking Powder and one teaspoon salt. Chop one-quarter pound, or one-half cup of suet, quite fine, mix with flour, add enough cold water to make a stiff dough. Roll out and line a bowl with it. Cut up one pound of round steak in one-inch pieces, season with pepper and salt, and roll in a little flour. When bowl is half full of meat pour in one-half cup of water, add the rest of meat. Trim off crust and roll out a lid to fit on the top. Pinch the edges together, dip a cloth into boiling water, then in flour so it won't stick, cover over pudding, tie down and boil or steam for two and one-half hours. This may be boiled in a cloth but is not so good. Turn out to serve.

MRS. H. M. ROTH, ALBANY, N. Y.

Family Meat Loaf

Put one and a half pounds of round steak through food-chopper, also one onion. Soak stale bread in cold water (about one cup) squeeze out with the hands, add to beef, season with salt, pepper and celery salt; mix thoroughly. Five hard-cooked eggs may be used with this when they are cheap. Put a layer of the prepared meat in a bread pan, then a layer of the sliced eggs, meat and so on, having meat last. Turn into a dripping pan or covered roaster. Bake for one hour.

CONTRIBUTED.

Beef Loaf with Pimentos

Put two pounds of round steak through meat-chopper, also three Larkin Pimentos (Spanish red peppers) and three Larkin Soda Crackers. Cook one-half cup of Larkin Rice in boiling water for ten or fifteen minutes, add pepper, salt, meat and one egg. Mix very thoroughly together and bake in covered roaster forty-five minutes, or steam in Larkin Steam Cooker for one hour.

MRS. T. LEWIS, FOSTORIA, OHIO.

Jellied Beef Loaf

Buy a soup bone with some meat on it (shank is the best), put in soup kettle, cover with cold water, add one onion, one carrot and a small bay leaf and simmer gently for several hours or until the meat will fall from the bone. When it is done, put a little of the liquor in a saucer to chill. If it does not "jell" add enough Larkin Gelatine to stiffen, season with pepper and salt. Pour in molds rinsed with cold water. The meat may be put through the meat grinder if preferred.

MRS. F. L. FAECHER, AUGUSTA, KANS.

Jellied Veal or Chicken

Cook in the same manner as Jellied Beef. Remove the bones, season and use sufficient Larkin Gelatine to stiffen. Directions come with each package.

LARKIN KITCHEN.

Beef Stew

Two pounds of beef, two tablespoons flour, one small carrot, one pint water, two teaspoons salt, one-fourth teaspoon pepper, two tablespoons suet or drippings, one onion. Cut meat into small pieces, roll in flour, put drippings into pan, shake until smoking hot, then put in meat and sear on every side, add boiling water. Stir until boiling. Add all the seasonings, cover the pan and simmer for one and one-half hours, or place in a fireless cooker for three hours. Serve with dumplings.

MRS. J. B. BONNEAU, CHICAGO, ILL.

Egg Dumplings

Sift two cups Larkin Flour with two teaspoons Larkin Baking Powder, one-half teaspoon Larkin Salt. Beat one egg light; add one-half cup of water; mix with flour, using spatula. Have broth boiling; drop in dumplings with a teaspoon; let them rest on the meat; cover tight and boil gently for twenty minutes without lifting the cover. If you follow this rule, you will have the lightest and tenderest dumplings you ever ate.

MRS. THOMAS MORGAN, PITTSTON, PA.

Potato Dumplings

Pare three medium-sized potatoes and boil until tender. Put through potato ricer or mash quite fine. Add to them one cup flour, one teaspoon salt, one egg lightly beaten. Handle as little as possible, roll out and cut in six squares. In the center of each put some bread-crumbs which have been crisped brown in the oven (a little minced onion is very good, added to the crumbs). Roll up the squares of dough around the stuffing, make into ball shape, drop into boiling water or broth and boil steadily for twenty minutes. Do not remove lid while cooking. These may also be steamed.

MRS. WILLIAM STARKE, METHUEN, MASS.

Nut Steak without Meat

Put into a mixing bowl one cup of walnut meats coarsely chopped, two cups of bread-crumbs, one-half teaspoon each of salt and dried sage, and a very little pepper. Mix dry ingredients together, add one egg slightly beaten and four tablespoons of milk. Shape as you would Hamburg Steak and sauté in hot frying pan with a small amount of fat. Serve with tomato sauce.

MRS. J. F. HILLMAN, TRENTON, N. J.

Beef Fritters

Put one pound of round steak through a Larkin Food-Chopper. Season with pepper and salt, then add one can of Larkin Corn, one cup of bread- or cracker-crumbs and two eggs slightly beaten. Cook the same as pork sausage in a hot frying pan.

MISS ORRIL NEWLAND, HOOPESTON, ILL.

American Chop Suey

Cook one-half package of Larkin Short-Cut Macaroni in boiling salted water for twenty minutes. While this is cooking put two onions and one-half pound of round steak through a Larkin Food-Chopper. Brown in a hot pan with a piece of butter or beef drippings. Drain water from macaroni, add one can of Larkin Tomatoes, season with Larkin Salt and Pepper, then add steak and onions and cook slowly for thirty minutes. Serve piping hot. This is sufficient for six persons.

MRS. JNO. PIERCE, LONSDALE, R. I.

Chili Con Carni

Put one pound each of veal and beef, also one large onion, through a Larkin Food-Chopper. Cover with water and simmer one and one-half hours. When almost cooked add one cup boiled Larkin Short-Cut Macaroni, one can Larkin Tomatoes and one can of Larkin Peas. Season with salt and red pepper. Will serve nine people.

MRS. H. H. BENTHEIMER, GREEN BAY, WIS.

Roast Pork

Wipe pork with a damp cloth, sprinkle with pepper, salt and flour. Put into covered roaster, leave off the cover first thirty minutes, then cover closely. Allow twenty minutes for each pound. Bake in a moderate oven. Make gravy as for beef. Apples, with the cores removed, may be placed around the pork to bake. This gives the pork an excellent flavor.

LARKIN KITCHEN.

Baked Pork Chops

Pare seven good-sized potatoes, slice as for scalloped potatoes. Take one and a quarter pounds of lean pork chops (loin preferred), put a layer of potatoes into a Larkin Casserole or Baking Dish, then a layer of pork chops, dust with salt and pepper, sprinkle with chopped onion, continue until all is used. Have potatoes on top. Pour in one cup of water or milk. Put on the cover and bake in moderately hot oven for one hour and forty minutes; uncover during the last ten minutes so potatoes will brown. Serve direct from the Casserole. Delicious.

MRS. WM. HESS, ST. LOUIS, MO.

Apple Fritters

Sift three times, one cup Larkin Pastry Flour, with three tablespoons sugar, one teaspoon Larkin Cream of Tartar Baking Powder, one-fourth teaspoon Larkin Salt; add one well-beaten egg, one-third cup milk and two tart apples, pared, cored and sliced. Drop into deep fat and fry until brown. Drain and sprinkle with sugar. The apples may be coarsely chopped and stirred into batter if preferred. Serve with roast pork.

MRS. A. E. HENDERSON, TWIN FALLS, IDAHO.

Larkin Sauerkraut

Put into a kettle one quart of Larkin Sauerkraut, one pound of fresh pork, two onions put through Larkin Food-Chopper and water enough to cover. Cook slowly three hours. The longer it is cooked the better, but it should be cooked almost dry when done.

MRS. ROY S. HEATWOLE, HARRISONBURG, VA.

Salt Pork with Cream Gravy

Cut required amount of pork in moderately thin slices. Place in spider and cover with boiling water, cook a few minutes, take out and dip each piece in milk, then in flour. Put a few spoons of pork fat in spider and fry the pork until brown. Dish on a hot platter. Stir two tablespoons of flour into the fat, add pepper and salt if needed, add to this one pint of milk, stirring until gravy thickens. Pour gravy over pork and serve with baked potatoes. Delicious.

MRS. H. WRENCH, GOODRICH, WIS.

Boiled Ham

Soak ham several hours or over night in cold water to cover. Wash thoroughly, put into a kettle, cover with cold water, heat to boiling point and cook slowly until tender, allowing twenty minutes to the pound. Remove from range and set aside so that ham may partially cool; then take from water, remove outside skin, sprinkle with fine brown cracker-crumbs and stick with cloves one-half inch apart. Or it may be covered with brown sugar and baked in the oven until brown. Cabbage and potatoes may be cooked in the water in which the ham is boiled and served with the ham as a boiled dinner.

LARKIN KITCHEN.

When Frying Ham

Slice and fry in usual way. Then over fried meat pour hot water and immediately pour off again. This freshens the ham and leaves it tender and delicious. Use the water, which is rich in meat flavor, to make the gravy. Larkin Bacon may be cooked in the same way.

MISS CHARLOTTE BIRD, ANN ARBOR, MICH.

Deviled Ham and Eggs

Put bits of ham through a Larkin Food-Chopper. For one cup of ham, put into a frying pan one tablespoon of butter, add one tablespoon of Larkin Flour, one teaspoon of vinegar, Larkin Pepper, and a fourth of a teaspoon Larkin Mustard and one-half cup of water. Let it boil, then put in the minced ham. Stir until very hot, turn into a pie dish or casserole and break on the surface five raw eggs. Put in the oven and bake five minutes or just long enough to set the eggs. Serve in baking dish.

MRS. C. FLINN, NORTH TERRE HAUTE, IND.

Pork Sausage

Chop very fine one pound or two cups of cold cooked pork, moisten a slice of stale bread in half a cup of water, add to it the pork and three or four tablespoons of mashed potatoes, and one beaten egg, season with salt, pepper and sage. Mix well and shape into small flat cakes with the hands; dust lightly with flour or rolled cracker-crumbs, and sauté in a little hot fat.

MRS. SIDNEY R. LODDER, SYRACUSE, N. Y.

Good Sausage Meat

When making pork sausage use one-third fat and two-thirds lean. Put through food-chopper and, to every twelve pounds of pork, take twelve teaspoons salt, six teaspoons pepper, nine teaspoons sifted sage. Mix well with the hands and put through the food-chopper again. Keep in a cool, dry place.

MRS. E. THOMAS, BRISTOL, CONN.

Pork Sausage with Tomatoes

Separate one pound of link sausage, pierce each sausage several times with a fork. Place in hot frying pan. Cook until brown. Add one-half can of Larkin Tomatoes and one cup of water; also one tablespoon each of onion and parsley finely chopped. Add pepper and salt. Cook twenty minutes. The gravy may be thickened if preferred. Sufficient for six people.

MRS. GEORGE CLANSZ, PEARL RIVER, N. Y.

Sausage Rolls

Make pastry as for pie-crust, using one and a half cups of Larkin Pastry Flour, one-half cup Larkin Pure Lard and one-half teaspoon Larkin Salt. Mix with cold water. Roll out and cut in small squares. Put one piece of Larkin Luncheon Sausage on each square, and pinch the edges together. One can of sausage makes eight of these rolls. Brush over with white of egg and bake in a hot oven. Very delicious for lunch when serving Club-of-Ten. Fresh pork sausage may be used if it is either parboiled or baked in the oven before using.

MRS. H. WRENCH, GOODRICH, WIS.

To Cure Hams, Bacon and Dried Beef

For every twenty pounds of meat use three-fourths of a pound of Larkin Salt, one-half ounce saltpeter, and one cup Larkin Molasses, mixed thoroughly. Rub meat with mixture, keep it in the brine for three days, skin side down, repeat rubbing process until it has been done three times. Put in the smoke for three days after last rubbing. MRS. EDW. THOMAS, BRISTOL, CONN.

Roast Veal

The leg and loin are most suitable for roasting. Wipe meat with a damp cloth, sprinkle lightly with Larkin Salt and Pepper, dredge with flour. Place slices of salt pork over and around meat. Veal is best cooked in covered roaster. If cooked in an open pan, baste often. Make gravy as for beef. LARKIN KITCHEN.

Veal Loaf

Put one and one-half pounds of veal through the food-chopper with one-half pound of salt pork, also eight Larkin Soda Crackers and two or three sprigs of parsley. Add Larkin Pepper, Salt and two tablespoons lemon juice, also two eggs slightly beaten. Bake in a greased bread-pan one hour in a moderate oven. Baste occasionally if necessary. MRS. H. F. RIEMER, DETROIT, MICH.

Sweetbreads

Sweetbreads spoil very quickly. Remove from the paper as soon as received. Put into cold water, add a little salt, leave for one hour, drain, cover with boiling water, add a little salt. Cook slowly twenty minutes, drain and cover with cold water, so that they may be white and firm. To broil; cut in slices, sprinkle with salt and pepper, dip in bread-crumbs, sauté in frying pan. Serve with green peas. LARKIN KITCHEN.

To Roast Poultry

One rule will apply to all poultry.

Have oven very hot until skin is browned, then cool, and if poultry is stuffed, cook twenty minutes to the pound; unstuffed, fifteen minutes. Salt pork is very nice to use for basting purposes; baste frequently if in open pan. A covered roaster is much to be preferred as no basting is then required. LARKIN KITCHEN.

Fried Chicken

Singe, clean and cut in pieces ready to serve, dip in cold water, drain but do not wipe; sprinkle with salt and pepper and dip in flour. Cook in hot pork fat or Larkin Cooking Oil, serve with gravy made in the pan with milk. LARKIN KITCHEN.

Maryland Chicken

Dress, clean and cut up a chicken; sprinkle with salt and pepper; dip in flour, egg and crumbs; place in well-greased dripping pan and bake in hot oven, basting with butter or other fat. Arrange on platter and pour over it two cups cream sauce.

LARKIN KITCHEN.

Pot-Roast Chicken with Dumplings

Cut up the chicken, wash and dip in flour, brown in hot fat, cover with boiling water, add pepper, salt and one carrot and one onion if liked. Cover kettle so all the flavor will be retained, simmer until tender. If an old fowl it will take two or three hours. When almost tender add one cup of Larkin Rice or drop in dumplings ten minutes before serving. Do not remove the cover after the dumplings are in or they will be heavy.

MRS. GEORGE CLANSZ, PEARL RIVER, N. Y.

Chicken Pie

Cut up a chicken as for stewing, cover with boiling water, add pepper and salt, cook until tender. Remove the large bones and place chicken in a baking dish, slightly thicken the gravy. Do not have the baking dish more than three-fourths full. Make a good biscuit dough and cut in rounds as for biscuits. Place the biscuits over the chicken leaving room for the steam to escape. Bake in hot oven until thoroughly done. This is an improvement over the old style crust as the biscuit is more easily served and never becomes soggy. MRS. R. E. BEST, DECATUR, ILL.

Chicken, Creole Style

Chop fine, one green pepper, one onion and two large tomatoes, or use one and one-half cups of canned tomatoes. Put some butter or other fat in a sauce-pan, add the onion and pepper and cook until soft, but not brown. Brown the chicken, then cover it with boiling water, add the tomatoes and simmer until tender (if an old fowl, about two hours). Sprinkle one cup of washed rice over the chicken, put on lid and cook another half hour. This is very delicious. Veal or mutton may be used in place of chicken. MRS. G. NOMDEDEN, BALTIMORE, MD.

Extra Dressing for Chicken

In making an extra supply of dressing this is a nice way to fix it. Scrape out the inside of two half-loaves of bread, leave the crust thin. Rinse out the inside with cold water and fill with the extra dressing. Invert on pie tin and bake about forty-five minutes. This will be found very nice.

MRS. ANDREW RICHARDS, PERRINTON, MICH.

Dressing for Geese, Ducks and Pork

Chop, or finely slice, four onions, cook until soft, drain off the water, add two cups of bread-crumbs, one teaspoon dried sage, salt and pepper to taste.

MRS. HORACE ANDERSON, DOVER, N. J.

Rabbit en Casserole

Skin, wash and cut up one or two rabbits, cover with cold water and stew thirty minutes. Roll in flour, season with salt and pepper and brown in frying pan. Put into a Larkin Casserole, add chopped onion, sprinkle with flour, add sufficient water, made slightly acid with mild vinegar, to cover. When rabbit is prepared in this way it loses the peculiar flavor many people object to. You will find this a very delicious dish. Bake one hour or more. Serve from the casserole.

MRS. R. W. SLEETER, ROCKFORD, IOWA.

Fried Rabbit

Skin, wash and cut up two rabbits. Cover with cold water and cook until tender. The water should not boil, only simmer. Roll the rabbit in seasoned flour and brown in hot fat. Use the liquor in which they were cooked, for making gravy.

LARKIN KITCHEN.

Rabbit in Covered Roaster

Clean and joint a rabbit, roll in flour, season with pepper and salt. Add a slice of pork cut up in small pieces. Place in covered roaster, add one pint of boiling water, put on the cover and bake for one hour in medium oven. Then add potatoes and bake another forty-five minutes. This may also be cooked in the same fashion as a pot roast.

MRS. JOSEPH LARDIFF, DULUTH, MINN.

Filled Cabbage Leaves

Separate the leaves of a medium-sized cabbage, pick out the best, pour over them boiling water, leave for a few minutes. Cook one-half cup rice, mix with it one pound Hamburg Steak, add one-half teaspoon Larkin Onion Extract, salt and pepper to taste. Line a kettle with the outside cabbage leaves. Fill the scalded leaves with the prepared meat. Roll up; lay closely together in kettle so they will not separate. Add one teaspoon salt, a little pepper, three-fourths cup canned tomatoes, three tablespoons bacon fat or butter, and water to almost cover. Put on the lid. Cook gently thirty minutes. Remove the filled leaves, add one egg beaten light, and the juice of one lemon to the liquor in the kettle. Stir until thick, but do not allow to boil or it will curdle. Pour sauce over cabbage leaves and serve at once.

MRS. WM. SCHNEIDER, BUFFALO, N. Y.

Stuffed Cabbage

Wash a cabbage weighing about four pounds. Tie in a cloth and cook in boiling salted water until wilted. Take out and lay on a platter; turn back the leaves. Cut out the heart and place in a chopping bowl with four hard-boiled eggs, and one pound of pork sausage. Season with salt and black pepper, chop fine. Make a ball, place in center of cabbage, fold over the leaves one at a time, tie up in the same cloth, and boil gently for one and one-half hours.

MRS. EDITH WILSON, GRAND ISLAND, NEBR.

COLD MEAT COOKERY

Beef with Tomatoes

Two cups of chopped cold meat, one cup of canned tomatoes, one cup of cracker- or bread-crumbs, salt and pepper. Put a layer of meat in a baking dish, and over it a layer of tomatoes, then a layer of cracker-crumbs, next a layer of meat and so on until dish is filled. Bake about thirty minutes.

MRS. THERESA SCOFIELD, AMSTERDAM, N. Y.

An Economical Meat Dish

Take any left-over meat, chicken, beef, or pork, cut into cubes. Heat in gravy or a white sauce, well seasoned. Put meat in center of platter, surround with a can of heated Larkin Pork and Beans. Garnish with parsley or celery tips. This uses up scraps of meat you would sometimes throw away, and, combined with the nutritious beans, it may be used as the main dish for luncheon or supper.

MRS. S. E. RICHARDSON, TOPEKA, KANS.

"Different" Hash

Put any cold meat on hand through a Larkin Food-Chopper. To two cups of the cold meat allow one-half pound of fresh round steak, put this through the food-chopper also. Cut up one large onion in small pieces, put some drippings into the frying pan; when quite hot put in the onion, brown thoroughly and add the chopped raw beef, dust with salt, paprika and celery salt. When this is brown, add the cooked meat to it. Prepare raw potatoes as for potato chips and fry in another pan, drain and salt. Then add to the hash. Pour over some gravy if you have it, if not use water. Pack the hash down in the pan and cook over a moderate fire about ten minutes. Place a dish or round plate over the pan and turn out. You will then have a beautifully browned, savory meat dish. This is a little more trouble than the ordinary hash but it is worth it.

MRS. H. ARMBRUSTER, BROOKLYN, N. Y.

Michigan Hash

One pound of Hamburg Steak, two tablespoons of chopped onion, one cup cooked Larkin Rice and two cups cooked Larkin Macaroni. Rice and macaroni may be hot or cold. Place in layers in baking dish; season each layer with Larkin Salt, Black Pepper and Celery Salt. Pour strained tomatoes over all until quite moist, sprinkle with cracker-crumbs and bake forty-five minutes in moderate oven. MRS. ROWE, FORT SMITH, ARK.

Casserole of Rice and Meat

Put three cups of cold cooked meat and one-half onion through Larkin Food-Chopper, add salt and pepper, two eggs slightly beaten and two tablespoons bread-crumbs. If you have any soup stock on hand, add sufficient to moisten well; if not, use milk. Butter a mold, line with boiled rice, then add layer of meat, then rice and so on until dish is filled. Have layer of rice on top. Cover closely and steam forty-five minutes. Serve with brown gravy or tomato sauce.

MRS. L. W. KINNEY, LAKE CHARLES, LA.

Turkish Rice

Boil or steam three-fourths cup of Larkin Rice until tender. Then add two tablespoons of butter, mix thoroughly, and place on back of stove. Heat one pint of strained tomatoes, add soda the size of a pea, one tablespoon of sugar, salt and pepper to taste. Put two cups of cold chicken, veal, or beef through Larkin Meat-Chopper, add meat and tomatoes to rice and mix thoroughly. May be prepared several hours before using.

MRS. THOS. E. LEWIS, FOSTORIA, OHIO.

Minced Beef

Put scraps of cooked meat through Larkin Food-Chopper, season with pepper and salt, place in a frying pan with a spoonful of butter and enough water to moisten. While this is heating, toast pieces of stale bread a light brown. Dilute one tablespoon of flour with a little milk and mix with the meat. Pour over each piece of toast and serve at once.

MISS CARRIE STELTZER, GRANVILLE, PA.

Chicken Cutlets

Season pieces of cold chicken or turkey with salt and pepper. Dip in melted butter; let this cool on the meat, and dip in beaten egg, then in fine bread-crumbs. Fry in hot fat until a delicate brown. Serve on slices of hot toast, with a cream or curry sauce. Pieces of cold veal are nice prepared in this way.

MRS. DAVID DAVIES, REMSEN, N. Y.

Chicken Hash with Noodles

Put left-over chicken through Larkin Meat-Chopper, add one cup of gravy or a Larkin Bouillon Cube dissolved in one cup of hot water. Take one-quarter of a pound or one cup of Larkin Egg Noodles, cook in boiling water for ten minutes, drain, then add two cups of Larkin Tomatoes, two teaspoons of sugar, pepper and salt to taste. Put into Larkin Casserole or Baking Dish, with the chicken, sprinkle top with cracker- or bread-crumbs. Bake in moderate oven for one-half hour.

FRANCES B. HAUSER, ROCHESTER, N. Y.

Ham Surprise

Take two slices of Larkin Ham (cold boiled) cut in medium-sized pieces. Make a batter with one egg, one-half cup of milk, a pinch of salt, a teaspoon of Larkin Baking Powder, and sufficient flour to make a smooth batter, (not too thick). Dip piece of ham in batter and fry a delicate brown in hot fat

MRS. B. P. MONAHAN, BRIDGEPORT, CONN.

Salmagundi

Cook for twenty minutes in boiling salted water, two cups of Larkin Short-Cut Macaroni. Drain, blanch in cold water. Have ready about half a pound of cold cooked beef, cut in cubes. Put into a Larkin Casserole, a layer of macaroni, then a layer of meat, a layer of sliced onion, then a layer of tomatoes (either canned or fresh). Dust over a little salt and pepper and dot with butter. Continue layers until all is used up. Have a layer of cracker-meal on top. Pour over any gravy you have, if not sufficient, use a little milk or water. Bake forty-five minutes. This is delicious and makes a good hearty meal.

MRS. JAMES A. CUMMINGS, GOUVERNEUR, N. Y.

Savory Hash

Prepare a dressing as suggested in Mock Duck. Mix with two cups or one pound of cold, cooked beef, veal or pork. Mold in a bread pan, turn into a dripping pan, add a few slices of bacon or pork, or drippings. Bake slowly forty-five minutes. Serve with tomato sauce or brown gravy.

MRS. M. G. ROWE, FORT SMITH, ARK.

Escalloped Potatoes

Pare and dice amount of raw potatoes needed. Butter a baking dish, put in layer of potatoes, sprinkle with flour and salt. Add another layer of potatoes and continue as before, until pan is three-fourths full. Then add sufficient cream to cover (milk and butter may be used in place of cream). Bake in hot oven for forty-five minutes. They should be brought to a boil quickly or the milk may curdle.

MRS. IRVEN RYSTROM, STROMSBURG, NEBR.

Cheese Potatoes

Put a layer of sliced cold potatoes into a baking dish, then a layer of cracker-crumbs, pepper and salt to taste, and specks of butter and cheese. Add another layer of potatoes and so on until all are used. Sprinkle grated cheese on top. Cover with milk and bake twenty-five minutes in a hot oven.

MRS. BERNICE BEESON, GREENFIELD, IND.

Potatoes au Gratin

Put a layer of diced cold potatoes into a baking dish, season with salt and pepper, cover with alternate layers of white sauce and diced potato. Cover the top with buttered bread-crumbs, sprinkle with grated cheese and bake in a quick oven about twenty-five minutes.

MRS. JOHN SIMARD, AMHERST, MASS.

Onion and Potato Hash

Chop fine two small onions, fry in meat drippings, when about half done add two or three cups of cold potatoes cut in dice. Stir all together, season with salt and pepper.

MRS. FRANK HASTINGS, SARANAC LAKE, N. Y.

Potato Patties

Mash cold potatoes smooth with a fork. Add one tablespoon of flour, a little butter, salt and pepper; work all together and pat into thin round cakes. Fry in hot fat. Delicious for breakfast or supper.

MRS. HARVEY CHAMBERS, MAYSVILLE, KY.

Stuffed Potatoes

Select six smooth potatoes of uniform size, wash clean, wipe and put into hot oven to bake. When thoroughly baked, cut in halves, scoop out the inside, take care not to tear shells, mash potato smooth, add one-half cup cream, two tablespoons butter, and one teaspoon of Larkin Peanut Butter. Salt to taste. Beat light, fill in shells, put into a baking pan and bake a light brown. Serve hot. If desired these can be prepared some time before needed, bake when ready to serve.

Mrs. W. L. Umbarger, Konnarock, Va.

Potato Puffs

Beat two cups of hot mashed potato until smooth. Stir in one beaten egg, one teaspoon grated onion and a little milk if needed. Season to taste with salt and pepper. Drop by spoonfuls on a buttered baking sheet. Bake in a quick oven until light and brown.

Mrs. H. W. Rowe, Waterville, Maine.

Walnut Sweet Potatoes

Peel and boil until tender, twelve sweet potatoes. Cut in quarters, place in a baking dish, baste with butter, sprinkle with sugar and black walnuts coarsely chopped. Bake in moderate oven until brown.

Mrs. Winnie Howells, Murphysboro, Ill.

Potato Fritters

Mix together two cups of hot potatoes put through vegetable ricer, or mashed very fine, two eggs beaten, four tablespoons flour diluted with a little milk, one-fourth teaspoon Larkin Salt. Fry in deep hot fat, about a dessert spoonful makes a nice size fritter, or form into small cakes and sauté in frying pan. If not thick enough, add a little more flour.

Mrs. Margaret R. Schutte, Tampa, Fla.

Boiled Turnips

Peel and slice the turnips. Cover with a generous amount of boiling water, cook until tender, not longer. If they are to be mashed, drain thoroughly and mash with a wooden potato masher. Season with salt, butter and pepper and serve at once. When cooking turnips, two things should be kept in mind: to add salt when cooked, and not to over-cook. Turnips cooked in salt water become pink and develop a bitter flavor.

Larkin Kitchen.

Peas in Turnip Cups

Hollow out the centers of small white turnips. Cut the edges in points, steam or boil gently until tender. Make a sauce with two tablespoons of butter, two of flour and one cup of milk, add salt and one-half cup of Larkin Green Peas. When quite hot fill the cooked turnips and serve one to each person.

MRS. JOHN BARTL, ROCHESTER, N. Y.

Baked Peas

Soak one quart of Larkin Green Peas over night. In the morning parboil and drain. Add two tablespoons of sugar, one-quarter teaspoon Larkin Pepper, two teaspoons Larkin Salt and one pound of salt pork. Bake in bean pot adding water as you would for baked beans. Bake slowly all day. Serve for supper with brown bread.

FLORENCE C. THAYER, STONEHAM, MASS.

To Boil Parsnips and Carrots

Scrape parsnips, cut in halves, put into cold water. When ready to cook, cover with boiling water and cook slowly until tender, about three-quarters of an hour. Drain, baste them with butter, sprinkle with pepper and salt and serve. Parsnips are very nice dipped in batter and fried in hot fat. Carrots and parsnips are good served in a cream sauce. Young carrots will cook in thirty minutes.

LARKIN KITCHEN.

To Cook String Beans

As you string and cut the beans, put them in cold water to keep crisp. When ready to cook, put the beans into a sauce-pan, add a piece of butter such as you would use to season them, and a very little water. Cook over a moderate fire, add salt and a little more water if needed. Keep the cover on during the cooking; add milk when done and serve hot. The beans will have an excellent flavor when cooked in this way.

MRS. A. B. DE LONG, CRESTON, IOWA.

String Beans with Bacon

Remove the strings from yellow or green beans and cut in one-inch pieces. Slice two small onions and a small piece of bacon, add a pinch of Larkin Cayenne Pepper, and a little Larkin Salt. Put into a sauce-pan, cover with boiling water and cook until tender. Let the liquor cook down before taking from the stove. The onion is not objectionable as so small an amount does not give a decided taste. This is a good substitute for a meat dish.

MRS. ELSIE SEACOY, BRAINERD, MINN.

To Boil Cabbage

Cut a small head of cabbage into four parts, cutting down through the stalk. Soak for half an hour in a pan of cold water to which has been added a tablespoon of salt—this is to draw out any insects that may be hidden in the leaves. Take from the water and cut into slices. Have a large stew-pan half full of boiling water; put in the cabbage, pushing it under the water with a spoon. Add one tablespoon of salt and cook from twenty-five to forty-five minutes, depending upon the age of the cabbage. Turn into a colander and drain for about two minutes. Put into a chopping bowl and mince. Season with butter, pepper, and more salt if required. Allow a tablespoon of butter to a generous pint of the cooked vegetable. Cabbage cooked in this manner will be of delicate flavor and may be generally eaten without distress. Have the kitchen windows open at the top while the cabbage is boiling and there will be little if any odor of cabbage in the house.

LARKIN KITCHEN.

Cabbage German Style

Cut the cabbage on a slaw cutter, put into a kettle, add salt and about four tablespoons meat drippings or butter, add sufficient water to keep it from burning. Cover closely and steam forty-five minutes until tender, but not soft. Beat one egg until light, add a cup of sour cream, and a little sugar. Mix with the cabbage; do not let it boil or the egg will curdle. Serve at once.

MRS. QUINCY R. SHERRY, CONNERSVILLE, IND.

Corn Fritters

One cup flour, one teaspoon salt, two eggs, one-half cup milk, one teaspoon melted butter, one-third teaspoon pepper, one teaspoon baking powder, two cups Larkin Canned Corn. Sift together the flour, salt and baking powder, in a bowl. Separate the eggs; beat yolks light, add the milk. Pour gradually into the flour mixture and stir to a smooth batter. Add butter and corn; cut and fold into the batter the stiffly-beaten egg whites. Fry by the spoonful in deep hot fat. Drain on soft paper. Serve at once. This batter may also be used for fruit and other vegetables fritters.

MISS DELIA TAGATZ, WAUTOMA, WIS.

Corn Oysters

Beat two eggs light, add one can of Larkin Corn, one tablespoon melted butter, and one-half cup of flour sifted with one-half teaspoon salt. Fry on hot griddle by the spoonful. Serve with cold meat or as a dessert with Larkin Maple Syrup or Honey.

MRS. BESSIE BINNALL, DOW CITY, IA.

Green Corn Pudding

Cut the corn from six nice fresh ears; add two beaten eggs, two tablespoons of butter, one-half teaspoon salt. Break up six Larkin Soda Crackers, cover with one pint of milk, leave for ten minutes, add to the other ingredients. Bake in moderate oven about twenty minutes or until nicely browned. This is fine.

MISS CARRIE STELTZER, GRANVILLE, PA.

Fried Tomatoes

Take solid tomatoes, not overripe, and slice in one-fourth-inch slices. Season with salt and pepper, dip into beaten egg and Larkin Cracker Meal. Fry in Larkin Cooking Oil or bacon fat until golden brown. Serve with bacon, ham or steak.

MRS. L. LOEFFLER, GLENDALE, L. I., N. Y.

Tomato Cakes

Beat four eggs light. Add one can of Larkin Tomatoes and three tablespoons melted butter, pepper and salt to taste. Stir in cracker-crumbs to make it stiff enough to drop by the spoonful on a hot greased griddle. Brown on both sides. Serve at once. Good for luncheon or supper.

MRS. MARY CHAPMAN, SANTA ROSA, FLA.

Tomatoes and Rice

Steam one cup of rice in three cups of water until tender, add one can of Larkin Tomatoes, one teaspoon salt, one-quarter teaspoon white pepper, a small piece of butter, two tablespoons of sugar and one grated onion. Bring to a boil, serve hot. Will taste better if left standing for one hour before serving.

MRS. JOHN M. FORD, LUCAS, KANSAS.

Larkin Special

Cut up one slice of Larkin Ham and three onions, in small pieces. Cook together in frying pan, add one can of Larkin Tomatoes, pepper, and salt to taste, and when boiling, add one-half box of Larkin Noodles. Cook for twenty-five or thirty minutes. Serve hot.

MRS. MARY E. WEST, GLOUSTER, OHIO.

Boiled Rice

Pick over one cup of rice, put into strainer and wash thoroughly. For one cup of rice allow two quarts of boiling water, add one tablespoon salt. Have the water boiling rapidly during the entire time of cooking. Boil for fifteen or twenty minutes, if the rice is old it takes longer to cook. Drain in colander, pour over it one quart of hot water, place on oven door or back of range to dry off.

LARKIN KITCHEN.

Steamed Rice

Put three cups of boiling water into Larkin Double-Boiler No. 210. Sprinkle in one cup of rice which has been washed and drained, add one teaspoon salt. Steam for thirty minutes. Serve with milk or cream and sugar. Milk may be used in place of water, if desired. LARKIN KITCHEN.

Baked Rice

To serve with chicken or as a vegetable. Wash one cup of rice, drain and put into a buttered dish or casserole, add one-half teaspoon of salt, pour two and one-half cups of water over it. Cover and bake in a quick oven one-half hour. Uncover and steam dry. Lay slices of Larkin Bacon over the top, place in oven until brown, serve hot. MRS. PHILIP GOKEY, MOOERS, N. Y.

Rice Croquettes

Take one and a half cups of cold cooked rice or one-half cup of uncooked rice and steam in double sauce-pan, when tender add a beaten egg, one teaspoon onion juice or one-half teaspoon Larkin Onion Extract, one-half teaspoon salt and a dash of cayenne pepper and ground nutmeg. Mix thoroughly together, spread on a shallow plate to cool. When cold cut in small squares, dip in cracker-crumbs, beaten egg then cracker-crumbs again. Fry in hot fat. Dish on hot platter, garnish with green peas. This makes a very attractive supper dish.

MRS. FLORENCE G. CHIPMAN, ATTLEBORO, MASS.

Rice and Pimentos

Boil one cup of Larkin Rice in salted water until tender, chop fine one-half can of Larkin Pimentos. Slice thin or grate one-fourth of a pound of Larkin Cheese. Beat two eggs light, add one and a half cups of milk, two teaspoons Larkin Salt and one-quarter teaspoon Black Pepper. Mix altogether and bake in moderate oven twenty minutes.

MRS. STARL D. COOK, LANSING, MICH.

Spanish Peppers

Prepare six large sweet peppers. Boil one cup of Larkin Rice until soft, add one-half pound chopped round steak, dice six slices of Larkin Bacon, add a little chopped parsley, salt and pepper to taste. Mix thoroughly and fill the peppers. Strain one can of Larkin Tomatoes, add a little water and sugar, a pinch of cloves and cinnamon. Stand the filled peppers in a baking dish, surround with the tomato sauce and cook gently until soft (about twenty-five minutes). Rice, bacon, salt, pepper, tomatoes, sugar, cinnamon, and cloves were all bought from Larkin Co. MRS. C. ADAMS, HARRISBURG, PA.

Stuffed Green Peppers

For eight good-sized peppers, use one pint of cold boiled halibut or any other white fish. Mix with a white sauce made of one and one-half tablespoons of butter, one tablespoon of flour and one-half pint of milk. Season with Larkin Pepper and Salt and a few drops of Worcestershire Sauce. Add one raw egg slightly beaten, cook for two minutes, and fill prepared peppers. Put bread-crumbs and small pieces of butter on top and bake in hot oven twenty minutes.

MRS. A. J. LAWALL, NEWARK, N. J.

Stuffed Sweet Peppers

Six large peppers, one pint of tomatoes, one cup bread-crumbs, one large onion, one teaspoon salt, one-fourth teaspoon celery salt, one-fourth teaspoon pepper, one tablespoon butter. Remove top and seeds and soak the peppers in salt water for two hours. Mix together tomatoes and bread-crumbs, grate half of the onion, add seasonings, mix thoroughly and stuff the peppers. Place in a baking pan with the rest of the onion cut in small pieces. Add a little pork fat or butter and a very little water. Bake slowly one-half hour, basting often.

MRS. W. A. TINDALL, MARYVILLE, MO.

Baked Beans

Take one pint of Larkin Pea Beans, soak over night in cold water. Drain and add enough cold water to cover, put on fire and when they begin to boil, drain off water, add cold water as before, also one small onion chopped fine, one teaspoon salt and two or three slices of Larkin Bacon. Cook until beans are almost done, add two tablespoons of Larkin Canned Tomatoes, two tablespoons Larkin Molasses, and a pinch of Larkin Soda. Put in covered baking dish, arranging slices of bacon on top, and sprinkle with pepper. Bake four or five hours, adding hot water as needed to keep moist.

MRS. B. P. MONAHAN, BRIDGEPORT, CONN.

Baked Beans with Meat

Cover one quart of Larkin Dried Beans with cold water and soak over night. Drain, add water to cover, parboil until skins crack when blown on. Drain the beans and cover the bottom of Larkin Double-Boiler No. 210, three inches deep with beans. Add one large onion, one-half pound of salt pork and one-half pound of fresh pork (shank is good). Add remainder of beans, two tablespoons molasses, maple syrup or brown sugar, also a little salt. Add the strained juice from one can of tomatoes. Boil gently all day until supper time.

BELLE D. ROBINSON, WILLIAMSTOWN, VT.

A New Supper Dish

Take one can of Larkin Pork and Beans, four potatoes, one onion finely chopped, one-half teaspoon Larkin Celery Salt, one-fourth teaspoon Larkin Pepper. Cut each potato in four pieces, put all ingredients into sauce-pan. Add two cups of boiling water; cook thirty minutes. Serve hot. Sufficient for five people. Cheap and nourishing.

MRS. J. K. FOSTER, SEAFORD, VA.

Chafing-Dish Special

Put two tablespoons butter in the chafing-dish, add one cup of Larkin Pork and Beans which have been mashed thoroughly through a sieve. Add gradually one cup of milk; when quite hot and well blended add one cup of diced cheese or scraps of dry cheese grated. Two tablespoons of Larkin Chili Sauce improves the flavor and should be added with the cheese. It is ready to serve when the cheese is melted.

MRS. LESLIE E. BUSHNELL, NEW LONDON, CONN.

Baked Lentils

Soak two cups of dry lentils over night. In the morning drain and add one quart of hot water. When the water boils the lentils will rise to the top. Lift out with a skimmer and put them in a Larkin Casserole or a Baking Dish. Place a quarter of a pound of salt pork in the center of the lentils, and one small onion. Mix three teaspoons salt and fourth of a teaspoon of pepper with two cups of boiling water. Add to lentils. The lentils must be kept moist. If necessary add a little more water during the cooking. Bake in a moderate oven six to ten hours, or in a Larkin Fireless Cooker ten hours.

LARKIN KITCHEN.

Lentil Croquettes

Soak one cup of lentils and one-half cup of Larkin Red Beans over night, drain, add two cups of water. Cut up one small onion, one small head of celery, one small carrot, and three sprigs of parsley. Cook until quite soft, then press through a sieve, add one cup of bread-crumbs, one beaten egg, salt and pepper to taste. Make a sauce by creaming together three tablespoons of butter and three tablespoons of flour, add two-thirds of a cup of cream, (Larkin Evaporated Milk may be used). Stir until boiling, add to lentil mixture. Mix thoroughly, cool, shape, dip in egg and crumbs and fry in Larkin Cooking Oil. Drain on soft paper. Serve at once.

MRS. JOHN A. CONOVER, GAMBRILLS, MD.

Lentil Stew

Pick over and wash one cup of lentils, soak over night in a quart of water. The next morning put them on the fire and simmer in the water in which they were soaked. This will take about three hours. Add any vegetables you have on hand. I use a small onion and one potato. A little left-over meat or gravy or both added to stew during the last half hour gives it a delicious flavor. Cut the meat into small pieces. Keep just enough water on lentils so they will not burn. Add salt, pepper and butter to taste, before serving. We have this meal instead of meat at short intervals and find it very satisfactory. To cook with ham or corned beef prepare in the same way, using more water.

Mrs. W. R. Young, No. Tonawanda, N. Y.

A Good Supper Dish

Boil one cup of lentils as directed in recipe for Lentil Stew. Boil an equal quantity of rice. While these are cooking, prepare a pint of sauce by using two cups of Larkin Canned Tomatoes, a small piece of bay leaf, a fair-sized onion chopped fine and a blade of mace. Cook slowly for thirty minutes, then thicken with two tablespoons flour blended with three of butter. Carefully add the hot stock. Boil for a few minutes, then pour over the lentils and rice. Place the rice around the edge of platter and pile the lentils in the center. Will serve four or five people.

Larkin Kitchen.

Potato Salad

Cut six medium-sized cold boiled potatoes, three hard-boiled eggs, one onion, and one head celery, in small pieces, and mix thoroughly with boiled dressing. Serve on lettuce hearts; garnish with small radishes.

HELENA E. PIERSON, NORWOOD, R. I.

Vegetable Salad

Two cups cabbage, one cup celery, one cup cucumbers, one large onion, one cup cold boiled potatoes, three hard-boiled eggs, all finely cut, and two green peppers cut in rings. Serve with boiled dressing on lettuce leaves.

MRS. H. J. MOORMAN, LAWRENCEBURG, IND.

Combination Salad

Chop fine two sweet peppers, five good-sized apples, four pieces or stalks of tender celery. Remove the pulp from six tomatoes and add it to the other ingredients. Mix with salad dressing. Fill the tomato shells with the mixture. Serve on lettuce leaves.

MRS. JNO. P. GRANT, DELAWARE, OKLA.

Larkin Tomato Salad

Put two teaspoons Larkin Gelatine to soak in one-half cup cold water. Heat one can Larkin Tomato Soup, add one teaspoon salt, a dash of cayenne, a few drops Larkin Onion Extract. Add the softened gelatine; mold in small cups. When firm serve on lettuce leaves with Larkin Salad Dressing.

MRS. AUGUST HALBERSLABEN, MADISON, WIS.

Cabbage Salad

Cut a hard cabbage into halves and then with a very sharp knife shred fine the desired quantity; as you shred it put it into a bowl of very cold water and leave for two hours. It will be more crisp if you change the water once or twice. When ready to serve, put into a cloth and swing around until dry. Mix with simple dressing and serve at once, or the cabbage will lose its crispness. Celery may be added if liked.

MRS. G. K. GARRETT, PEQUEA, PA.

Combination Cabbage Salad

Soak one-half package Larkin Gelatine in one-half cup cold water for a few minutes, add one quart boiling water, one cup vinegar, juice of one lemon, one-half cup sugar and one teaspoon salt. When cold add two cups cabbage shredded fine, one and one-half cups celery cut fine and one-fourth can Larkin Pimentos cut fine. Pour into small teacups. When firm serve on lettuce with a spoonful of whipped cream into which has been stirred sufficient Larkin Salad Dressing to flavor. When preparing this just for ourselves, I pour it into a meat pan and cut in squares to serve. This should be served with the meat course.

MRS. J. C. CLARK, KNOXVILLE, IA.

Cream Slaw

Slice or chop one quart of cabbage, keep in cold water until ready to serve. Put one-fourth cup vinegar, one and one-half tablespoons sugar, and four tablespoons butter into a sauce-pan on the fire. Beat one egg light, mix with one tablespoon flour, add one cup sweet cream, salt and pepper. Add the hot vinegar to this, cook until thickened and pour over the crisp cabbage. Serve at once.

EVA M. K. KINDALL, SO. PASADENA, CALIF.

Simple Dressing for Cabbage

A very good dressing to serve with cabbage is whipped cream, either sweet or sour, into which has been stirred sufficient vinegar to make it tart, and a little sugar, salt and paprika. Do not mix with the cabbage until serving time. This dressing is also good with lettuce.

MRS. G. K. GARRETT, PEQUEA, PA.

Bean Salad No. 1

Drain liquor from one can Larkin Red Kidney Beans, add one head of celery or three chopped onions. Chop four hard-boiled eggs, one dozen small sweet pickles, and one cup nut meats. Mix all together and add hot mayonnaise made as follows: Yolks of four eggs, one-half cup sugar, scant cup weak vinegar, two teaspoons Larkin Corn Starch, four tablespoons butter,—salt and pepper to taste. Bring to a boil, stirring constantly.

MRS. KOOCH WILSON, ATTICA, IND.

Bean Salad No. 2

Empty one can Larkin Red Kidney Beans, rinse with cold water. Add one cup Larkin Stuffed Manzanilla Olives cut in small pieces, and one cup diced celery. Mix all thoroughly and serve with Larkin Salad Dressing on lettuce leaves.

MRS. WALTER R. HOLLOWAY, MURPHYSBORO, ILL.

Bean Salad No. 3

One can Larkin Pork and Beans, two cups of diced boiled ham, one good-sized Spanish onion, one large sweet green pepper, a little salt and pepper. Mix all thoroughly and when ready to serve, place on a bed of lettuce leaves and cover with good dressing. Hard-boiled eggs may also be placed on top. This is a very fine dish for a Sunday night tea.

MRS. GEO. S. BRAIN, JERSEY CITY, N. J.

Salad Delight

Wash one cup Larkin Rice; put on to cook in two quarts boiling salted water. Cook until tender but do not allow it to become too soft. Drain, and pour one quart boiling water through the rice. Dry on the oven door shaking occasionally to keep separated. Allow two tablespoons rice to one tablespoon salted ground almonds. Place on lettuce leaves, cut four oranges in small pieces, cover with sugar to form juice. Put one tablespoon juice with several small pieces of orange, over rice. Then add one tablespoon cream salad dressing. Place a very thin slice of orange on top and a salted almond on the orange. Serve with tea and wafers for a lunch at a Club-of-Ten party.

FLORENCE THAYER, STONEHAM, MASS.

Miscellaneous Salad

One-quarter pound mild cheese cut in small pieces, or grated; add three-fourths cup chopped sweet pickles, one cup chopped celery, and one cup broken walnut meats. Add sufficient boiled dressing to mix.

MISS R. JACOBS, PALMYRA, MO.

Chicken Salad No. 1

Cut cold boiled chicken in dice, add an equal amount of celery cut fine and one cup blanched almonds cut in halves. Season with salt and pepper. Stir into this a few tablespoons mayonnaise; set away for an hour or more. Just before serving, arrange on lettuce leaves and cover with thick mayonnaise. Garnish with celery tips, Larkin Olives, and Pimentos cut in strips.

MRS. SADIE CHAMBERLAIN, PONTIAC, ILL.

Chicken Salad No. 2

One cup chicken meat cut in small pieces, one cucumber cut in cubes, one cup English walnut meats broken in pieces, one-half can Larkin Peas, and two cups celery cut in strips. Mix with a silver fork, add one cup good salad dressing. Serve very cold in nests of lettuce. Garnish with Larkin Pimentos cut in points.

MRS. JNO. HAUSER, ROCHESTER, N. Y.

Chicken Salad No. 3

Mix together one can Larkin Deviled Chicken and twice the amount of crisp chopped cabbage. Add one-fourth teaspoon Larkin Celery Salt. Use a good salad dressing, serve on lettuce leaves.

MRS. ERNEST C. THURMOND, ASH GROVE, MO.

Salmon Salad No. 1

Flake one can Larkin Salmon, add four medium-sized cooked potatoes cut in cubes, four Larkin Pickles cut into small pieces, two cups finely-cut cabbage. Make a dressing with yolks of two eggs beaten light, one teaspoon salt, pinch of pepper, one teaspoon sugar, two teaspoons Larkin Mustard, one tablespoon butter, and four tablespoons Larkin Vinegar. Put into a Larkin Double-Boiler, stir until thickened, cool, add sufficient milk to thin out. Serve on lettuce leaves.

SARAH E. BURNS, SWATHMORE, PA.

Salmon Salad No. 2

Six hard-boiled eggs chopped fine, two mashed potatoes, one can Larkin Red Alaska Salmon, four sour pickles chopped fine. Mix all together with a good boiled dressing flavored with Larkin Celery Salt.

MRS. NETTIE L. RANEY, TULLAHOMA, TENN.

Marshmallow Salad

Cut up one-half pound Larkin Marshmallows, pour over them one-half can Larkin Pineapple, grated. Stand this aside several hours. Then add three sliced bananas, one-fourth pound chopped walnut meats, two oranges cut in pieces, add one-half cup whipped cream. Serve on crisp lettuce leaves. This is delicious.

MRS E. F. ALBRECHT, JAMAICA, N. Y.

Fruit Salad Supreme

One-half package Larkin Gelatine and pink coloring powder. One-half cup cold water. Three cups freshly-boiled water. Juice of one lemon. One cup sugar. Three bananas. Two oranges. Moisten gelatine in cold water, add sugar, juice of lemon, pink coloring powder and boiling water. Put half of this into mold. When this begins to set, slice the bananas and arrange them in it. Then take the other half which has started to set and beat until light and fluffy as whipped cream. Pour this on the first half and arrange the oranges cut in sections on the top. Any canned fruit may be used in place of fresh.

MRS. PERCY S. MACUMBER, CORNING, N. Y.

Fruit Salad No. 1

Peel and dice three bananas, one orange, and one small apple. Cut in cubes one-half can Larkin Pineapple. Chop one-half cup English walnut meats, add one cup Larkin Canned Peaches, and three tablespoons cherry preserves. Mix all together using a silver fork, sprinkle one cup granulated sugar over the fruit. Thicken the fruit juice with corn starch, allowing one tablespoon corn starch to one cup of juice. Add sugar if needed and one tablespoon butter; when quite cold pour over the fruit. Serve on lettuce leaves or in sherbet glasses for dessert.

MRS. M. E. BARLOW, FARMINGTON, ILL.

Fruit Salad No. 2

Four bananas, two oranges, three apples, one-half can pineapple, one-half cup English walnuts, one cup marshmallows. Cut the fruit, nuts and marshmallows in pieces, and mix all together (except the nuts). Add nuts just before serving as they turn the salad dark if put in too soon. Mix with cream dressing and serve on crisp lettuce leaves.

MRS. BERNICE BEESON, GREENFIELD, IND.

White Grape Salad

Halve and seed one pound white grapes. Cut up quite fine the best part of two heads of celery and the meat from one-half pound English walnuts. Mix with cream or French salad dressing. Serve on crisp lettuce leaves.

MRS. FRANK S. MERRILL, BRISTOL, CONN.

Cherry Salad

Stone one-half pound cherries, saving all juice. Dice a small cucumber, chop fine a dozen blanched almonds. Cook together until slightly thick, one cup cherry juice, two tablespoons lemon juice, and one-half cup sugar. When cool add two drops Larkin Almond Extract and when quite cold add to the salad mixture, mixing gently with two silver forks. Serve on crisp lettuce leaves. Canned cherries may be used when fresh ones are not in season.

MRS. FRANCES HAUSER, ROCHESTER, N. Y.

Pineapple Salad

One can Larkin Sliced Pineapple. One head of crisp lettuce, one bottle Maraschino cherries. Make a nest of two blanched lettuce leaves on individual salad plates. Put one slice of pineapple on each plate, cover with cream salad dressing, and put a cherry in center of each piece. Sprinkle with ground walnuts. This is a very pretty salad and most delicious. Canned Bartlett Pears with a sprinkling of lemon juice, may be substituted for the pineapple.

MISS EVA L. DAVIDSON, CHERRYVALE, KANSAS.

Banana Salad

Remove skins and cut in half lengthwise as many bananas as are needed, allowing one-half banana for each person. Mix Larkin Salad Dressing with whipped cream, roll banana in the dressing, then in chopped nuts. Walnuts, peanuts, or pecans, may be used. Serve on a lettuce leaf. A small spoonful of the dressing may be placed on the side of the plates and also two Larkin Saltines.

MRS. JNO. HYLER, PLAINFIELD, N. J.

September Salad

Pare, core and chop two ripe apples and one sweet red or green pepper. Add one cup diced celery, two tablespoons chopped onion, two teaspoons finely chopped parsley, and one cup Larkin Shredded Cocoanut. Mix thoroughly. Serve with French or cooked salad dressing in tomato shells or on lettuce leaves.

MRS. PEARL M. HACKER, COUNCIL BLUFFS, IA.

Tomato Surprise

Peel three tomatoes and carefully scoop out the centers. Place them upside down to drain. Wash, dry and cut in one-inch pieces, four sticks of celery from a firm stalk. Break six eggs into a large bowl; beat quite light. Add to them one-half teaspoon Larkin Salt, a few grains of Cayenne Pepper, one-half teaspoon Larkin Onion Extract, four tablespoons milk. Pour into buttered pan and cook as for scrambled eggs. When cooked, add the celery and the tomato pulp cut in small pieces. Fill the tomato with the mixture and serve on lettuce leaves with Larkin Salad Dressing.

MRS. R. E. THOMSON, BUFFALO, N. Y.

Lobster Salad

Open one can Larkin Lobster and turn out on a china dish. Cut into cubes. Add three hard-boiled eggs coarsely chopped. Mix two tablespoons Larkin Salad Dressing with one cup whipped cream. Mix ingredients carefully together. Serve on lettuce leaves, garnish with three half slices of tomatoes. Sprinkle with finely chopped sweet green peppers and serve with Larkin Saltines.

LARKIN KITCHEN.

Meat Relish No. 1

To three quarts chopped cooked beets, take one quart raw cabbage chopped, one cup grated horseradish, two cups sugar, one tablespoon Larkin Salt. Mix all thoroughly, put in a jar and cover with cold vinegar. This is easy to make and very good.

MRS. W. C. OBENDORF, STERLING, ILL.

Meat Relish No. 2

Take one-half can Larkin Pimentos, three cups cabbage, nine sour pickles, two small onions. Squeeze out the vinegar from the pickles and put all the ingredients through a Larkin Food-Chopper. Mix together one teaspoon salt, one-half cup sugar and one-half cup vinegar (or vinegar and water mixed, depending on the strength of the vinegar). Stir all together and leave for one hour before serving. Excellent with cold meat.

MRS. K. K. HAGGSTROM, CHEYENNE, WYO.

Tomato and String Bean Salad

Scald and remove skins from six firm tomatoes, cool, cut a slice off one end and gently scoop out inside. Have one pint of fresh string beans boiled in salted water and cut in small pieces. Mix with tomato pulp. Make a dressing with one tablespoon of oil, two tablespoons vinegar, one teaspoon Larkin Tomato Catsup, one-half teaspoon salt, one-eighth teaspoon pepper. Add to this one tablespoon Larkin Gelatine; dissolve in one-half cup boiling water. Mix well, cool, add to string beans, and fill tomato cases. Put away on ice a couple of hours before using. Serve on lettuce leaves with mayonnaise.

MRS. A. J. LAWALL, NEWARK, N. J.

Cooked Dressing

Stir together one tablespoon Larkin Dry Mustard, one tablespoon Larkin Corn Starch, three tablespoons sugar, one teaspoon Larkin Salt, a few specks of Larkin Cayenne Pepper and a pinch of Larkin Soda. Add two well-beaten eggs, one cup milk, one tablespoon butter, and lastly (beating constantly) one cup weak vinegar. Cook until thick and creamy, stirring all the time.

MRS. JOHN H. FITZPATRICK, OLD CHATHAM, N. Y.

Uncooked Dressing

Stir together one teaspoon Larkin Prepared Mustard, two teaspoons sugar, one-half teaspoon salt, and one-quarter teaspoon Larkin White Pepper. Add one cup Larkin Evaporated Milk; mix thoroughly, then slowly add three tablespoons Larkin Vinegar. Mix well and it is ready for use.

MRS. GEO. RAUPP, BUFFALO, N. Y.

Dressing for Cabbage

Mix together one teaspoon sugar, one-half teaspoon Larkin Mustard, one-half teaspoon Larkin Salt and one beaten egg. Add four tablespoons vinegar and eight tablespoons cream. Cook until thick in a double-boiler, stirring constantly.

MRS. WM. NOLLER, TROY, N. Y.

Easy Mayonnaise

I have discovered that when oil dressing is made in the following manner it never fails. To the yolks of two fresh eggs, add one tablespoon vinegar, beat well, then add one-fourth teaspoon salt and one-half cup or more Larkin Olive Oil; beat constantly while pouring it in. The old-fashioned way is to drop the oil in very slowly but if the vinegar is added to the eggs first, the oil may be poured in much faster, and the mayonnaise will never curdle. Season with Larkin Celery Salt, Larkin Onion Extract, Mustard or any other seasoning you prefer.

MRS. MELVIN SMITH, AVON, N. Y.

Creamy Salad Dressing

Put into a double sauce-pan four lightly-beaten eggs, and one-half cup each of vinegar and water. Stir over the fire until thick, then add one-half cup butter. Mix together one teaspoon each of Larkin Mustard and sugar and a pinch of white or cayenne pepper. Add a spoonful of the cooked dressing to these seasonings and stir until smooth. Add balance of dressing and thoroughly mix. Thin with milk or cream as needed. Use more vinegar if liked quite sour. Whipped cream folded into this makes a very light dressing for salad. This will keep for weeks in a Mason jar if screwed down tight and left in a cool place.

MRS. EVA S. PUGH, BROWNELL, KANS.

Sue's Salad Dressing

Mix one teaspoon Larkin Mustard, one teaspoon sugar, and the yolks of two eggs. Add one-half cup vinegar and cook until thick. Then fold in the stiffly-beaten whites of two eggs. Cook for two minutes, cool, thin out with milk or cream as needed. The beaten whites insure a light, fluffy dressing.

MISS SUE MILLER, EDENVILLE, PA.

Peanut Dressing

Mix together in a small bowl two tablespoons Larkin Peanut Butter, two tablespoons lemon juice, two tablespoons cold water, one teaspoon Larkin Salad Dressing and one-eighth teaspoon Larkin Salt. This is a delicious dressing to serve on lettuce, onions, cabbage, etc.

MRS. ALEX. JACKSON, FAYETTEVILLE, N. CAR.

French Dressing

Rub a small bowl with garlic or onion, then put in one-half teaspoon Larkin Salt, one-fourth teaspoon each of Larkin White Pepper, Mustard, Sugar and paprika, add six tablespoons Larkin Olive Oil, stir in drop by drop two tablespoons Larkin Vinegar. If the oil floats, too much vinegar has been used.

LARKIN KITCHEN.

Mother's Salad Dressing

Cook three eggs until hard; cover with cold water. Take one-half can Larkin Evaporated Milk (Baby Size), slowly add one-half cup Larkin Cider Vinegar to the milk, one teaspoon salt, a dash of pepper and one tablespoon granulated sugar. Shell the eggs, cut in half, remove yolks and mash very fine. Add to above mixture. Cut whites of eggs into rings for garnishing. This is delicious on lettuce or raw cabbage.

MRS. CLAYTON E. HACKETT, MARSHALLTOWN, IOWA.

Dressing for Two

Put three teaspoons sugar, one-fourth teaspoon mustard, one-half teaspoon Larkin Celery Salt and a little pepper into a bowl, add one egg, beat until thoroughly mixed. Now add three tablespoons vinegar, one tablespoon each of butter and water, cook in double sauce-pan until thick. When cool thin with milk or cream.

MRS. CORA EDWARDS, MEMPHIS, TENN.

Salad Suggestions

A person with ingenuity will make a salad with whatever happens to be on hand. Here are a few suggestions:

Equal parts of white grapes (seeded) and diced bananas.

Juicy apples and oranges, cut in dice. Add a few Maraschino cherries.

Hard-boiled eggs, celery and English walnuts.

Apples, oranges and blanched almonds.

Marshmallows, walnuts and pineapple.

Tuna Fish, celery and boiled dressing.

Chopped beets, cabbage and hard-boiled eggs.

Cabbage and apples, boiled dressing.

To Boil Eggs

Eggs are cooked in many ways, but for cooking in the shell there is no better way than to put the egg into one pint of boiling water, cover, stand in a warm place, leave for six minutes, when the eggs will be cooked through, but soft; if liked very soft, allow less time. Be sure to have enough water, according to the number of eggs; if two eggs are needed use one quart of water, and so on accordingly. To cook eggs hard leave them in the water for thirty-five minutes. Then put them in cold water for five minutes.

LARKIN KITCHEN.

To Turn and Fold an Omelet

Tip pan so as to bring one side of omelet higher than the other. Place spatula under higher side and tipping pan to almost a vertical position, carefully fold over. If a half-inch cut is first made at each end of fold, the omelet folds more easily and without breaking.

LARKIN KITCHEN.

Poached Eggs

Have a shallow pan nearly full of boiling salted water, remove scum and reduce temperature until water is motionless; break an egg into a saucer and slip into the water; when a film has formed over the yolk and the white is firm, take up with a skimmer and place on toast which has been trimmed into shape. A much easier way is to use Larkin Double-Boiler and Egg-Poacher which poaches five eggs at one time.

LARKIN KITCHEN.

French Omelet

To four eggs allow three-fourths cup cold water,—salt and pepper to taste. Beat the eggs very light, then add the water and thoroughly mix. Pour into hot greased frying pan, run spatula around the edges and lift slightly to allow the thin part to run underneath. Serve at once on a hot platter.

LARKIN KITCHEN.

Puffy Omelet

Separate three eggs; with the yolks, put a little pepper, salt and one tablespoon cold water; beat the whites to a stiff froth; lightly mix in the yolks. Make a pan rather hot, grease lightly, pour in the mixture, cook three minutes on hot stove, then place in a hot oven and cook until just setting; fold over and turn onto a hot platter. If your oven is not hot turn the omelet carefully over and finish cooking on top of stove. Minced ham, or beef, with a tablespoon chopped parsley, is very good, either stirred into the mixture or placed on the top. Grated cheese is very nice sprinkled over the omelet just as you put it in the oven.

LARKIN KITCHEN.

Corn Omelet

Use rule given for puffy omelet. Fold in one-half cup canned corn; take care not to stir the mixture.

LARKIN KITCHEN.

Bread-Crumb Omelet

Separate the whites and yolks of three eggs. Beat the yolks light, add to them one-half cup fine bread-crumbs, one-fourth teaspoon salt, a few grains of pepper and one-half cup milk. Then fold in the stiffly-beaten whites. Put two teaspoons butter into a smooth frying pan, when hot pour in the omelet and cook over a slow fire. Use a Larkin Spatula to turn the omelet or put into hot oven to finish the cooking. Fold into a half circle and serve at once as any egg mixture falls if left standing.

BERTHA A. BOTTNER, PETROLIA, PA.

Stuffed Eggs

Boil six eggs twenty minutes. Cover with cold water for five minutes. Shell the eggs, cut in halves, remove yolks, add to yolks one teaspoon Larkin Prepared Mustard, a few specks of Larkin Black Pepper, one-half teaspoon salt, one tablespoon butter, and sufficient milk or cream to moisten. Fill each hollow where yolks were removed. Arrange on lettuce leaves and garnish with chopped beets.

MRS. B. P. MONAHAN, BRIDGEPORT, CONN.

Savory Eggs

Chop fine one small onion and one tomato. Cook in frying pan in small amount of fat until brown. Separate four eggs, add to the yolks one-half teaspoon salt, a dash of cayenne pepper, and two tablespoons cold water. Beat the whites lightly, mix with the yolks, add to the tomato in the frying pan and cook gently, as for scrambled eggs. Serve on buttered toast.

MRS. G. NOMDEDEN, BALTIMORE, MD.

Spanish Eggs

Cook six eggs until hard, remove shells, cut in halves lengthwise, take out and mash yolks smooth. Add three teaspoons melted butter, three Larkin Sardines rubbed to a paste, a dash of cayenne pepper, and one-half teaspoon salt. Mix and form into a ball and fill the hollow in each white. Have ready one cup cooked rice. Pile up in center of a platter, sink the eggs into the rice, and pour over the eggs and rice two cups seasoned cream sauce. Garnish with parsley, serve very hot.

Mrs. J. Allison, Pearl River, N. Y.

Delicate Eggs

Lightly toast two slices of bread, spread with butter, trim off the crust. Beat the whites of two eggs until quite light, spread on the toasted bread, drop the yolks in the center, sprinkle with pepper and salt, bake until slightly brown in a medium oven. Serve at once.

Mrs. E. Thomas, Houtzdale, Pa.

Eggs with Tomato Sauce

Put two tablespoons bacon fat into a frying pan. When melted add one small chopped onion. Cook until brown, then add one cup Larkin Tomatoes. Dilute two tablespoons flour with one cup water; add to above mixture. Season with one-half teaspoon salt, cook three minutes. Break four eggs into the sauce. Cook until set; serve on toast with the sauce poured around.

Mrs. A. DeScenza, Medford, Mass.

Scalloped Eggs

Boil six eggs twenty minutes, shell, cut in thin slices and place in baking dish a layer of eggs then a layer of cracker-crumbs. Sprinkle with pepper and dot with butter. Continue this until eggs are all used. Pour over the whole one cup cream or rich milk. Bake twenty minutes.

Mrs. Lenora Gant,
Minneapolis, Kans.

Macaroni is an excellent food, wholesome, delicious and digestible. Larkin Macaroni contains a large amount of nutriment in the form of starch, protein, and mineral matter, as only the best flour obtainable is used.

It is thoroughly dried before packaging, so that there is practically no loss in weight. It is truly an economical article of diet and can be prepared in a great variety of ways. This wholesome food should be found more often on our tables.

If macaroni lacks flavor it is due to improper cooking. Follow directions given and so get best results.

To Cook Macaroni

Partly fill a large kettle with water, adding one teaspoon salt to each quart of water. When boiling, put in the macaroni and boil rapidly for twenty-five or thirty minutes. Stir occasionally with a spatula or wooden spoon, drain through a colander, rinse with cold water, drain again and it is ready for use.

When Larkin Macaroni is cooked in this way it will be firm and white and have a delicious flavor.

Macaroni may also be cooked in a double-boiler. Allow two cups of boiling salted water to each cup of macaroni. It will take thirty minutes to cook. No starch is lost when this method is used, as all the water is absorbed by the macaroni. Cheese, tomatoes, milk and eggs all combine with macaroni to make delicious dishes. It may also be served plain-boiled with a little butter, and used in place of potatoes with any meat.

LARKIN KITCHEN.

Custard Macaroni

Cook one cup Larkin Short-Cut Macaroni in boiling salted water until tender. Drain. Beat two eggs, add one pint milk and three-fourths cup grated cheese, a sprinkling of pepper and a pinch of salt and soda. Put the Macaroni into a baking dish, add the cheese custard. Bake in a moderate oven for one-half hour or until set. Serve for supper.

MRS. J. HERBERT ROBINSON, WASHINGTON, D. C.

Macaroni with Cheese

Cook one-half package Larkin Short-Cut Macaroni in boiling salted water until tender. Drain. Put a layer in the bottom of a well-buttered baking dish, over this spread Larkin Cream Cheese cut in small pieces, add bits of butter and a sprinkling of Larkin Soda Cracker-crumbs, then more macaroni and so on, filling the dish. Pour over this one scant cup cream or milk. Scatter buttered crumbs over the top. Bake half an hour or until nicely browned on top.

Mrs. Ernest C. Thurmond, Ash Grove, Mo.

English Style Macaroni

Cook one cup Larkin Short-Cut Macaroni in boiling salted water until tender. Rinse with cold water. Make a sauce by melting three tablespoons butter in a double-boiler. Add three tablespoons flour. When bubbling add one and one-half cups sweet milk. Stir constantly until thickened, add two-thirds cup grated cheese or four ounces cheese thinly sliced. Stir until melted. Add one-half teaspoon salt and a little pepper. Mix together sauce and Macaroni, reheat in kettle or put into baking dish and bake about twenty minutes until brown.

Mrs. I. F. Knee, Omaha, Nebr.

Italian Macaroni

Cook one-half package Larkin Short-Cut Macaroni in boiling salted water. Season one pound chopped raw beef with salt, pepper, and Larkin Onion Extract and cook as Hamburg Steak. Slice one small onion and fry with the steak. Put the macaroni on the serving dish and the steak on top. Add a little flour to the fat in the frying pan and one-half can Larkin Tomatoes. Season with salt, pepper and one-half teaspoon sugar. When cooked pour the sauce over meat and serve at once. Grated cheese may be sprinkled on top. Place in oven until melted. These quantities will serve five people.

Carrie Jordan, Belvidere, Ill.

Macaroni with Meat

Put one-half package Larkin Short-Cut Macaroni and one cup Larkin Egg Noodles into boiling salted water and cook until tender. Put one-fourth pound salt pork through Larkin Food-Chopper. Try out the pork in a spider, then add three sliced onions and one pound ground steak. Cook until brown. Drain Macaroni and Noodles, add to contents in spider, also one can Larkin Tomatoes, one teaspoon each of sugar and salt, one-fourth teaspoon white pepper. Cook forty-five minutes. No potatoes will be needed.

Mrs. Carl Southworth, Bridgewater, Mass.

Macaroni and Oysters

Cook two cups Larkin Short-Cut Macaroni until tender and drain. Have ready one and one-half dozen fresh oysters. Put a layer of Macaroni in bottom of baking dish or casserole, then a layer of oysters and so on with Macaroni on top layer. Cover with a cream sauce made with two tablespoons melted butter, add two tablespoons flour; when bubbling add gradually one cup hot milk and the liquid from the oysters. Stir until boiling. Season with salt, pepper and a dash of cayenne pepper. Pour sauce over oysters and Macaroni and bake about one-half hour. Do not cook a moment longer than necessary or the oysters will become tough. Serve in baking dish.

MRS. LEIGHTON, BROOKLYN, N. Y.

Macaroni with Sausage

Cook one-half package Larkin Short-Cut Macaroni in boiling salted water fifteen minutes. Drain. Put Macaroni into a baking dish or casserole, add one pound pork sausage cut in two-inch pieces, one can Larkin Tomatoes, one-half teaspoon Larkin Celery Salt, one-fourth teaspoon white pepper, thoroughly mixed. Bake in hot oven for forty-five minutes. Serve in baking dish.

(NO NAME GIVEN) LOWELL, MASS.

Macaroni and Salmon

Cook one cup Larkin Short-Cut Macaroni in boiling salted water until tender. Drain. Open one can Larkin Salmon; break Salmon apart with fork. Make a cream sauce with two tablespoons butter, one tablespoon oil drained from Salmon, three tablespoons flour, and two cups milk. Arrange the Macaroni and Salmon in layers. Season Salmon lightly with cayenne pepper and salt. Pour sauce over each layer. Sprinkle buttered crumbs over the top. Bake in hot oven thirty minutes.

MRS. ARTHUR HOLTOM, TIFFIN, OHIO.

Nilson Macaroni

Cook one-half package Larkin Short-Cut Macaroni in boiling salted water. Cut up three slices Larkin Bacon in small pieces, cook until crisp, add three or four onions thinly sliced and fry until brown; then add one can Larkin Tomatoes, one teaspoon salt, a pinch of soda and a little cayenne pepper. Mix with macaroni, put into a baking dish, bake in a hot oven for twenty minutes.

MRS. H. B. VON NILSON, OMAHA, NEBR.

Dried Beef with Macaroni

Cook one cup Larkin Short-Cut Macaroni. Separate one-fourth pound dried beef. Put layers of beef and Macaroni into baking dish, cover with two cups seasoned cream sauce. Sprinkle buttered crumbs over the top and bake thirty minutes in a moderate oven.

MRS. WALTER MILLER, NEWARK VALLEY, N. Y.

Cheese Balls

To two cups grated cheese, add one-fourth teaspoon salt, a few specks of cayenne pepper and the stiffly-beaten whites of three eggs, or sufficient of the egg-white to moisten the cheese. Form into balls, roll in bread-crumbs, fry in hot fat. Serve in nests of lettuce as a luncheon dish. The cheese may also be made softer with more egg and dropped on Larkin Saltines or rounds of thin toast and baked slowly until firm.

MRS. JOHN H. WELLS, NASHVILLE, TENN.

Cheese Fondu

Mix together one cup milk, one cup soft, fine bread-crumbs, one-half cup grated cheese. Add one lightly-beaten egg. Season with one-fourth teaspoon salt and a pinch of cayenne pepper. Put into a buttered baking dish, bake twenty minutes in moderate oven. Serve at once.

MRS. KARL E. NOYES, SALISBURY, VT.

Cheese Puff

Put one-half box Larkin Butter Crackers through a Larkin Food-Chopper with one-half pound cheese. If you have no dried crumbs put a crisp, brown bread-crust through also, but keep the bread-crumbs separate. Season mixture lightly with cayenne pepper and salt. Put into a buttered baking dish and pour in sufficient milk to come to the top of dish. Let stand for twenty minutes so the cracker-crumbs will absorb the milk. Sprinkle the bread-crumbs on top, dot with butter. Bake twenty minutes in a moderate oven. Serve immediately. This dish costs twenty cents and will serve six people.

MRS. JNO. HYLER, PLAINFIELD, N. J.

Welsh Rarebit

One tablespoon butter, one teaspoon Larkin Corn Starch, one-half cup thin cream, one-half pound mild cheese, one-fourth teaspoon each of salt and Larkin Mustard, a few grains of Larkin Cayenne Pepper. Melt the butter, add corn starch, stir until well mixed, then add cream gradually and cook two minutes. Add cheese and stir until melted. Add seasonings. Serve on toasted bread or Larkin Crackers.

MISS MAUD E. BRYANT, HAVERHILL, MASS.

Cheese Fingers

Cut the crusts from thin slices of bread. Spread a slice lightly with creamed butter, then a layer of cheese, slightly seasoned with Larkin Salt and Pepper; cover with a second slice of bread. Then cut into finger-lengths, about one inch wide, using a sharp knife. Place in shallow pan and brown in hot oven. Serve with soup or a green salad.

MRS. ANDREW WILHELM, EASTON, PA.

Southern Golden Fleece

With a fork break up one-half pound Larkin Full-Cream Cheese. Put into a baking dish in a warm oven. When soft, add one cup cream and a sprinkling of Larkin Cayenne Pepper; blend thoroughly with a silver fork. Break over this five eggs, sprinkle with salt, cover with a plate, place in oven for a few minutes and when the whites begin to set beat briskly for several minutes, then put back in the oven and cook for three minutes. If properly cooked it will be light and fluffy like an omelet. Serve immediately it is done. Heat Larkin Butter Crackers in the oven and pass with this. Delicious as a supper dish for company.

MRS. OSCAR PRESTEGARD, PRATT, MINN.

Blushing Bunny

Put into a Larkin Chafing Dish two tablespoons butter; when melted, add two tablespoons flour. Pour on gradually one cup thin cream or milk; when thickened add one-half can Larkin Tomato Soup and one cup macaroni which has been cooked in salted water; then add one-half pound cheese, grated or thinly sliced, and two eggs slightly beaten. Season with salt and a little Larkin Cayenne Pepper and Mustard. This is sufficient for a party of six girls and is delicious.

CHARLOTTE B. RICHARDSON, TOPEKA, KANS.

Bread Made with Compressed Yeast

Sift together three quarts Larkin Bread Flour, add three teaspoons Larkin Salt, add one cake compressed yeast softened in one-third cup of lukewarm water, and one quart cool boiled water. Mix thoroughly, sprinkle the bread-board with flour and turn dough onto it. Knead until dough ceases to stick and is smooth and elastic to the touch. Then put into bread-raiser and let raise. It will take about three hours. Divide into four parts, mold each into a loaf, place in bread-pans, cover with a clean cloth and let raise again until double in bulk. Bake forty-five minutes in a moderate oven.

MRS. M. AMOROSA, ROCKLAND, MASS.

Bread with Potato Yeast

To prepare Potato Yeast boil six potatoes, mash very fine or put through a potato ricer. Pour one quart boiling water over one quart flour. Add the potato, one cup sugar, two tablespoons salt, and when cool, three cakes dry yeast which has been softened in one cup lukewarm water. Mix thoroughly and stand aside in a fairly warm place for several hours. Use one cup yeast to a quart of liquid. If kept air-tight in a cool place it will keep good for three or four weeks.

To make bread take one quart warm liquid, (milk or water), and one cup potato yeast. Stir in enough Larkin Flour to make a soft batter, set in a warm place to raise; when very light, add sufficient flour to make a stiff dough, knead very thoroughly, and place in four greased bread-pans. When light, bake in a moderate oven.

MRS. DANIEL WILLBY, SPRINGFIELD, MO.

Crisp Bread without Baking Powder

Sift one and one-half cups flour with one-half teaspoon salt. Chop or rub in one-half cup butter and lard mixed; add one tablespoon sugar. Mix with one cup sweet cream. Roll thin, lay in baking pan and score in strips about three-fourths of an inch wide. Bake in a hot oven. Serve with salad or coffee.

MRS. HOMER O. HASTINGS, ADENA, OHIO.

Milk-and-Water Bread

Put one tablespoon each of sugar, salt and lard into a quart measure, add two cups scalded milk, and two cups water. Mix thoroughly and pour into the Larkin Bread Maker, reserving sufficient to soften one cake dry yeast. When the yeast is quite soft, add to the liquid in the pan and sift in three quarts Larkin Bread Flour. Put in the kneading-rod and turn for three minutes. Cover and let raise over night. In the morning if a very fine bread is desired, put in the kneading-rod and stir again for a few minutes. Allow to raise, divide in four portions, mold, place in greased bread-pans, let raise again, then bake forty-five minutes in a moderate oven.

MRS. WM. G. TRIBON, SAGAMORE, MASS.

Old-Fashioned Bread

Boil and drain sufficient potatoes to make one pint, mash thoroughly, scald one pint flour with the liquid in which potatoes were boiled. Soften one cake dry yeast in one cup warm water, add three cups water, one tablespoon salt and one-half cup sugar to scalded flour. Beat thoroughly and allow to stand over night. In the morning, add flour to the batter and beat quite stiff with a wooden spoon. Let it raise, then add more flour, kneading the dough thoroughly. Again put to raise until double in bulk, divide into four portions, mold, place in greased bread-pans and, when quite light, bake in a moderate oven.

MRS. THELMA MILLER, OSCEOLA, IND.

Graham Bread or Buns

Scald one quart new milk, add one-half cup sugar, one-half cup Larkin Cooking Oil and one teaspoon salt; add one cake yeast softened in one-half cup warm water. Mix to a firm but soft dough, using equal parts of graham and white flour. Let the bread raise to double its bulk, cut off pieces of dough the size of a small egg, make into small flat cakes. Put into well-oiled pans two inches apart so they will not touch in raising. When quite light, bake in a hot oven. This may also be baked in loaves in the usual way.

MISS C. E. PUGH, BROWNELL, KANS.

Graham Loaf

Mix together two cups Larkin Graham Flour, one cup bread flour, and one-half teaspoon salt. Put one teaspoon soda in one-half cup molasses, mix thoroughly, fill up the cup with sugar, add to the dry ingredients with one and one-half cups sweet milk. These quantities make one large loaf. Bake one hour in moderately hot oven.

MRS. RAY F. COSSENTINE, SUSQUEHANNA, PA.

Larkin Oatmeal Bread

Put two cups Larkin Rolled Oats into bread-mixer, two teaspoons salt, scant one-half cup Larkin Molasses, three tablespoons lard, add one quart boiling water. When cool add one yeast cake softened in one-half cup luke-warm water. Add two quarts sifted Larkin Bread Flour, stand aside to raise or leave over night. In the morning stir down, add more flour if necessary. It should be stiff enough for the spoon to stand upright. It is well not to knead the bread with the hands as it is better a little moist. Put into three greased bread-pans, raise one hour. Bake forty-five minutes in a moderate oven. Whole-wheat or graham flour may be used instead of white flour if preferred.

Mrs. J. N. Jersey, Park Ridge, N. J.

Raised Corn-Meal Bread

Put one-half cup Larkin Yellow Corn-Meal into the bread bowl and pour over it one pint boiling water. Add one tablespoon Larkin Lard, one-half cup Larkin Molasses and one and one-half teaspoons Larkin Salt. Stand aside to cool. Soften one-half yeast cake in one-half cup warm water, add to mixture with enough Larkin Bread Flour to make a stiff dough. Knead well and set to raise. Next morning knead again and form into loaves; when quite light bake in a moderate oven.

Mrs. LeRoy A. Grant, Roslindale, Mass.

Southern Spoon Bread

Heat one quart milk to boiling point, stir in two cups Larkin Corn-Meal and one teaspoon Larkin Salt; add three tablespoons melted butter, and cook five minutes. Cool mixture. Separate three eggs, beat the yolks, add to the mixture, then fold in the stiffly-beaten whites. Pour into buttered baking dish or Larkin Casserole and bake in a moderate oven forty-five minutes. Serve while hot. This is especially good served with roast pork.

Mrs. H. Viger, Clarendon, Pa.

Boston Brown Bread

Sift together one cup Larkin Bread Flour, two cups graham flour, two cups corn-meal, add one cup molasses, three and one-half cups thick sour milk, two teaspoons soda and one teaspoon salt. Mix thoroughly, divide into three molds and steam one and one-half hours. Sweet milk and baking powder may be used instead of sour milk and soda. This bread is much improved by standing in a hot oven about fifteen minutes after it is steamed, to dry out.

Mrs. W. C. Obendorf, Sterling, Ill.

Nut Bread

Sift four cups flour with four teaspoons baking powder, one-half cup sugar, one teaspoon salt, add one cup chopped walnut meats, one egg lightly beaten, and one and one-half cups sweet milk. Put into two bread tins and stand aside to raise twenty minutes. Bake in a moderate oven forty minutes. Excellent for sandwiches.

MRS. N. L. HULL, TROY, N. Y.

Raisin Nut Loaf

Mix together one cup Larkin Graham Flour, one-half cup Larkin Bread Flour, one-half teaspoon salt, one-half cup sugar, and three tablespoons softened lard. Beat one egg light, put one teaspoon soda into one cup thick sour milk, add, with the egg, to dry ingredients, then stir in one-half cup each of chopped English walnut meats and raisins. Turn into greased bread-pan, stand aside thirty minutes before baking. Bake in a moderately hot oven forty-five minutes.

MRS. L. A. MINCKLER, OSHKOSH, WIS.

Corn-Meal Gems

Sift together one-half cup Larkin Bread Flour and one cup Larkin Corn-Meal, two teaspoons Larkin Baking Powder, one-half teaspoon Larkin Salt, and one tablespoon sugar. Stir in one cup milk, one well-beaten egg, and two tablespoons melted butter or lard. Beat thoroughly and pour into greased muffin-pans. Bake in a quick oven about twenty minutes. Buttermilk or sour milk may be used with good results.

LAURA J. SIGMAN, WATER VALLEY, MISS.

Baking Powder Biscuits

Sift together two cups Larkin Flour, one teaspoon salt and three teaspoons Larkin Baking Powder. Rub into the flour two tablespoons each of lard and butter. Mix to a soft dough with a three-fourths cup milk. Roll out one-half inch thick, cut into biscuits, place in a greased pan. Do not let biscuits touch. Brush tops with sweet milk, and bake from ten to fifteen minutes in a hot oven.

MINNIE BLOSSOM, WESTBORO, N. Y.

Cream Biscuits

Sift together three times, four cups Larkin Bread Flour, four teaspoons Larkin Baking Powder, and one teaspoon Larkin Salt. Add one cup heavy sweet cream and one cup sweet milk or use enough coffee cream to mix. Roll lightly, cut in biscuits and bake in a quick oven. This rule also makes an excellent crust for chicken pie, very tender but not rich.

MRS. JOHN H. FITZPATRICK, OLD CHATHAM, N. Y.

Egg Biscuits

Sift together two cups flour, two teaspoons baking powder, one-half teaspoon salt, one teaspoon sugar. Add one teaspoon melted butter to one-half cup milk and one egg beaten lightly. Mix with a spatula, handle as little as possible, roll and cut. Bake in a quick oven.

MRS. WM. STARKE, METHUEN, MASS.

Shamrock Rolls

Soften one-half cake compressed yeast in one-third cup lukewarm water. Cream together two teaspoons Larkin Sugar, one teaspoon Larkin Salt, and five tablespoons Larkin Lard; stir in one beaten egg, then add five cups Larkin Flour, one cup warm water, and the softened yeast. Beat thoroughly, cover and let raise. When set at night it is ready for mixing the next morning. When molding, allow a heaping teaspoon of dough for each roll. Do not knead the dough; simply cut it down with a knife and lightly form into balls. Brush each roll with butter, place in a flat pan, bake in a hot oven. If kept in the refrigerator, rolls may be made from dough three to five days after setting.

MRS. JAMES R. ABERCROMBIE, ST. JOSEPH, MO.

Egg Rolls

When the bread sponge is light, before you add flour to stiffen, take out two cupfuls and put into a mixing bowl. Pour two cups warm water or milk over one-half cup sugar, one teaspoon salt, and a two-thirds cup of lard, or part lard and part butter. Add this to the sponge with one quart of sifted flour and three lightly-beaten eggs. Stand aside until quite light, knead, roll out on a board, cut into shape; when light, brush over with white of egg, and bake in a hot oven fifteen or twenty minutes depending on the size. For a delicious sandwich split open and spread with Larkin Peanut Butter.

MRS. JNO. M. FORD, LUCAS, KANS.

Parker House Rolls

Scald one pint milk and pour it over one tablespoon each of butter and lard, two tablespoons sugar and one teaspoon salt. Stir these until dissolved. When just warm, add one yeast cake previously softened in one cup lukewarm water. Add from seven to eight cups flour. Raise until double in bulk. Knead and roll out one-half inch thick, cut with large biscuit cutter, put a piece of butter size of a pea in center of one half and fold over. Place in greased pan allowing sufficient space between rolls for them to raise without touching. Brush tops lightly with milk. Bake in a quick oven for twenty minutes.

MRS. EBEN H. ANDERSON, NORTHAMPTON, MASS.

Pop Overs

Sift one cup Larkin Bread Flour with one teaspoon salt into a mixing bowl. Take one cup milk, add enough to the flour to mix smooth. Drop in one egg (unbeaten), beat for two minutes, add balance of milk. Pour into very hot buttered cups or gem pans, and bake from thirty-five to forty minutes in a moderately hot oven.

MARIAN A. DAVIS, WESTGROVE, PA.

Egg Muffins

Sift together two cups Larkin Bread Flour, one tablespoon sugar, two teaspoons baking powder, one-half teaspoon salt. Add one egg well beaten, one cup milk and one tablespoon melted butter. Beat rapidly until very light. Bake in greased muffin-pans in a hot oven.

MISS R. JACOBS, PALMYRA, MO.

Date Muffins

Sift one-half cup each of Larkin Whole-Rye and Bread Flour with one-half teaspoon Larkin Salt and three teaspoons Larkin Baking Powder. Add one cup Larkin Graham Flour, two tablespoons Larkin Sugar, one egg beaten light and one cup milk. Stir in one-half cup chopped dates and one-half cup ground walnut meats. Bake in gem pans in a hot oven.

MRS. ARTHUR FELCH, SOUTH FRAMINGHAM, MASS.

Rye Muffins without Shortening

Sift together one cup each of Larkin Bread Flour and Whole-Rye Flour, one teaspoon Larkin Soda, one-half teaspoon Larkin Salt. Add one-half cup molasses and one cup sour milk. Have iron gem-pans very hot and bake in a quick oven. For richer muffins add one egg and four tablespoons of butter or lard.

MRS. GEO. W. BUTTS, PUTNAM, CONN.

Graham Muffins

Sift together one cup each Larkin Bread Flour, one cup Larkin Graham Flour, four teaspoons Larkin Baking Powder, one teaspoon salt, and four tablespoons granulated sugar. Beat one egg light, add one cup milk and two tablespoons melted butter. Mix with dry ingredients, bake in hot oven in buttered gem-pans twenty-five minutes.

MRS. MARY E. TORMEY, PINE PARK, N. Y.

Bran Muffins

Two cups bran, one cup Larkin Bread Flour, one-fourth teaspoon Larkin Salt, one teaspoon Larkin Soda, one and one-half cups sour milk. Mix in order given. Will make one dozen muffins. Eat three each day, and keep the doctor away.

MRS. MARSHALL K. OLDS, SURRY, MAINE.

Pumpernickel or Whole-Rye Muffins

Sift together one and one-half cups each of Larkin Pumpernickel and Bread Flour, three teaspoons Larkin Baking Powder, and one and one-half teaspoons Larkin Salt. Sift three times. Beat together two tablespoons cream (sweet or sour) and two tablespoons molasses and one-fourth teaspoon Larkin Soda. Add one and one-half cups sweet milk and the sifted dry ingredients. These quantities will make one dozen muffins. Bake in hot oven.

LILLIE J. BABCOCK, TERRYVILLE, CONN.

Scotch Scones

Sift together twice, two cups pastry flour, one-half teaspoon soda. Rub in four tablespoons butter (or lard), add one tablespoon sugar and one-half cup currants. Mix rather stiff with one cup sour milk. Roll out round and about one-half inch thick, cut in four pieces pie-shape, brush over with milk and bake in a hot oven. Caraway seeds may be used in place of currants if preferred.

MRS. M. WRENCH, GOODRICH, WIS.

Potato Scones

Sift together one and one-half cups flour, one teaspoon salt, and two teaspoons baking powder. Rub in one-fourth cup butter, add one cup warm mashed potatoes. Mix to a soft dough with one egg and as much milk as necessary. Divide into three portions, roll into rounds one-half inch thick and cut each in four. Bake in a quick oven or on a griddle. Split, butter and serve hot.

MRS. KATIE CREIGHTON, LONACONING, MD.

Plain Scones

Mix and sift two cups Larkin Flour, two teaspoons Larkin Baking Powder, one-half teaspoon Larkin Salt, two teaspoons softened lard, stir in one well-beaten egg and one-half cup milk. Bake in oven or on hot griddle. To use part graham flour or oatmeal makes a pleasant variety.

MRS. L. MCFALL, KEWANEE, ILL.

Raised Coffee Cake

Into Larkin Bread-Maker put one cup butter and lard mixed, and one cup sugar. Add one quart hot milk. When lukewarm, add two yeast cakes previously softened in warm water, also one pound cleaned currants, one and one-half teaspoons ground nutmeg, and three quarts flour. Put all into the mixer together, turn five minutes, put aside to raise; when light bake in three loaves. This cake is very fine for sweet sandwiches or church suppers. By omitting the currants and adding two eggs this recipe is excellent for doughnuts.

MRS. HENRY WEED, BETHEL, CONN.

Bread or Coffee Cake

Take one cup bread sponge raised with yeast, add one cup sugar, one egg, one cup butter and lard mixed, one teaspoon soda dissolved in one tablespoon lukewarm water, one teaspoon each of cinnamon, cloves and nutmeg, one cup seeded raisins chopped. Add enough flour to make a batter as stiff as for fruit cake. Mix thoroughly. Put into a well-greased baking-pan, let raise and bake in a moderate oven. More fruit adds to the quality of the cake. It will make an excellent pudding cut in squares, steamed a few minutes and served with a good sauce. It is nearly as good as plum pudding and more easily digested. It also makes a good fruit cake by adding currants and citron and will keep fresh indefinitely if wrapped in Larkin Waxed Paper and kept in a Larkin Cake Box.

MRS. WM. WRIGHT, HOWE, IND.

Dutch Apple Cake

Pour one cup scalded milk over one-third cup each of lard and granulated sugar; add one teaspoon salt. When lukewarm, add one yeast cake softened in one-half cup lukewarm water. Add two unbeaten eggs and three cups Larkin Bread Flour. Beat thoroughly with a wooden spoon, cover and set in a warm place to raise until it has doubled in bulk. Spread in two square greased pans, brush over with melted butter. Pare and core five apples, cut in eighths, press the sharp edges of the apples into the dough. Sprinkle with one-third cup granulated sugar mixed with one teaspoon Larkin Cinnamon and scatter over top two tablespoons Larkin Currants. Bake one-half hour or more in a hot oven. Cut in squares and serve hot with butter or sweetened and flavored whipped cream. Also good when cold.

WILBERTA MERRELL BLISS, SHREWSBURY, MASS.

Milk Toast

Heat the milk, add butter and salt and pour over toasted bread, or make a thin cream sauce, pour it over the toast and serve hot. Make brown-bread milk toast in the same way.

LARKIN KITCHEN.

French Toast

Beat two eggs slightly, add one-half teaspoon salt, and one cup milk; strain into shallow dish. Soak bread in mixture until soft. Cook on a hot, well-greased griddle; turn and brown on both sides. Serve for breakfast or luncheon, with a sauce or maple syrup.

LARKIN KITCHEN.

Sour Milk French Toast

Slice stale bread one-half inch thick. Make a batter with one-half cup sour milk, one egg, one-half teaspoon Larkin Salt, one-half teaspoon Larkin Soda, one teaspoon sugar, add enough flour to make a thin batter. Dip each slice in the batter and brown in a skillet with part lard and part butter, or use pork fat.

MISS KATHARINE SELLERS, GREENCASTLE, IND.

Sour Milk Griddle-Cakes

Sift two and one-half cups Larkin Bread Flour, one-half teaspoon Larkin Salt, one and one-quarter teaspoons Larkin Soda. Add two cups thick sour milk and one egg lightly beaten. Drop by spoonfuls on a hot greased griddle. When full of bubbles, turn and cook on the other side. Serve with butter and maple syrup.

MRS. J. S. MILLS, SOUTH ASHBURNHAM, MASS.

Griddle-Cakes

Sift two cups flour, one-half teaspoon salt, and two teaspoons baking powder. Add gradually one cup water or milk. Cook as other griddle-cakes.

MRS. J. F. ALSIP, TACOMA, WASH.

Bread-Crumb Griddle-Cakes

Soak two cups stale bread-crumbs in cold water, squeeze out the water, add one cup flour and one pint thick sour milk. Let the mixture stand over night. In the morning add one egg beaten very light, one teaspoon each of salt and soda. Add more flour or liquid if necessary. Cook as other griddle-cakes.

MRS. JNO. N. STUKMAN, FREDERICKSBURG, VA.

Rye Griddle-Cakes

Sift together one and one-half cups Larkin Whole-Rye Flour, two teaspoons baking powder, one-half teaspoon salt, one teaspoon sugar. Beat one egg light, add to it one and one-half cups milk, add gradually to the flour. Cook as other griddle-cakes. Serve with Larkin Honey or Maple Syrup.

MRS. A. J. SKELLIE, LITTLE ROCK, ARK.

Corn-meal Griddle-Cakes

Scald one cup corn-meal with one cup boiling water, beat until smooth, thin with one pint buttermilk, add one teaspoon salt, one egg beaten light, one teaspoon soda, and enough sifted flour to make a batter. Cook on hot greased griddle. If sweet milk, use baking powder.

MRS. IRVEN RYSTROM, STROMSBURG, NEBR.

Peanut Butter Griddle-Cakes

Sift together two cups flour, two teaspoons baking powder, one-half teaspoon salt. Add one egg and four tablespoons Larkin Peanut Butter. Beat vigorously, add two cups milk. Bake on a hot greased griddle.

MRS. JOS. E. CULVER, NEW HAVEN, CONN.

Buckwheat Cakes with Sour Milk

Put into the sifter one and one-fourth cups buckwheat flour, one-fourth cup white flour, one teaspoon salt and one teaspoon each of baking powder and soda. Sift twice, put into the mixing bowl, add one egg beaten light and two and one-half cups thick sour milk. Bake on hot greased griddle, serve with honey or maple syrup.

MRS. OSCAR PRESTEGARD, PRATT, MINN.

Buckwheat Cakes with Sweet Milk

Sift together twice, one cup each of buckwheat and Larkin Whole-Wheat Flour, three teaspoons baking powder and one teaspoon salt. Add enough sweet milk or water to make a thin batter. Cook as other griddle-cakes. Serve at once with Larkin Corn Syrup. When using white flour allow one teaspoon baking powder to one cup of flour.

MRS. L. LOEFFLER, GLENDALE, L. I., N. Y.

Waffles or Pancakes

Sift one and three-fourths cups flour with two teaspoons baking powder and one-half teaspoon salt. Add one and one-half cups milk, the beaten yolks of two eggs and one tablespoon melted butter. Fold in last the stiffly-beaten whites of the eggs. If you make waffles quite often it is well to buy a small can such as is used for oiling sewing-machines, fill with Larkin Cooking Oil and keep for oiling waffle irons.

Miss M. A. Kershner, Shoemakersville, Pa.

Potato Pancake

Pare and grate eight medium-sized potatoes, add one teaspoon salt, one well-beaten egg, and four tablespoons Larkin Bread Flour or sufficient flour to make a fairly thick batter. Mix well, drop a spoonful at a time into a hot greased frying pan, cook slowly until a golden brown, turn and brown the other side. Serve with butter. Will serve six people.

Mrs. Chas. F. Schaefer, Indianapolis, Ind.

German Pancake

Sift one-fourth cup flour with one-fourth teaspoon salt and one-half teaspoon baking powder. Beat two eggs quite light, add to them two cups milk. Mix gradually with the flour, pour into hot buttered iron pan. Lift the edges with a spatula so the batter may run underneath. If possible finish baking in hot oven. Roll up and turn out on a hot platter. Serve with lemon and sugar, or maple syrup.

Mrs. J. H. Westman, Strawberry Ridge, Pa.

There are two classes of cakes—sponge cake, in which no butter is used—and butter cakes. Sponge cake includes white, yellow and sunshine cake. Examples of butter cakes are: layer, cup, pound, etc.

In making cakes use the best materials. Flour must be sifted before measuring. Pastry flour is preferred. If bread flour is used, sift two or three times before measuring. Never melt the butter, the bowl may be slightly warmed before the butter is creamed. Larkin Cooking Oil or part lard and part butter may be used with good results.

Dried fruits should always be cleaned and well floured. Never wash currants just before using, or the mixture will be heavy. Add fruit at the last moment. If the fruit sinks to the bottom of the cake, the batter is too thin.

In making cake follow this order, first, get out all necessary utensils and materials, then ingredients. If using a coal range, arrange the dampers so that the oven will be ready by the time the cake is mixed. Next prepare the pans, then mix the cake. For butter cakes, grease the pan with oil, lard or butter, and dredge slightly with flour. For large cakes, line the pan with paper.

LARKIN KITCHEN.

Cakes without Butter

Sponge and Angel Food Cakes are raised by the air which is beaten into the whites of the eggs, and by slowly increasing heat of the oven. Care must be taken in combining the ingredients, not to stir the mixture or reverse the motion of beating or folding.

The flour and sugar should be sifted several times before being measured.

These cakes may be baked in ungreased pans if the pans are kept exclusively for them. The oven is right for these cakes when it turns a piece of white paper a light-brown in five minutes.

Angel food and sponge cake should be placed in a very slow oven, increasing the heat as it bakes, browning at the last.

LARKIN KITCHEN.

To Bake Cake

The oven should not be as hot for cake as for bread. It is right for cake baked in loaves if it turns a piece of writing paper a light-brown in five minutes. For layer and small cakes it should be hotter.

The time for baking a cake may be divided into four quarters:

First quarter: The cake rises; little bubbles form on top.

Second quarter: The cake continues to rise, and it browns in spots.

Third quarter: The cake browns all over.

Fourth quarter: The cake shrinks from the sides of the tin, becomes elastic to the touch, and stops singing.

During the baking, the oven heat should be increased gradually but very slightly until the cake is brown, then it may be slightly reduced. On the average a thin loaf will bake in forty minutes, while a thick loaf should bake for at least an hour. Fruit cakes may require several hours.

To turn cake out of the pan, loosen around the edges with a spatula and slip out on a wire cake-cooler or a clean towel or paper. If it sticks, turn it upside down, place damp cloth over the bottom of the pan and let it steam for a few minutes.

LARKIN KITCHEN.

Christmas or Wedding Cake

One pound of butter, one pound brown sugar, ten eggs, six cups flour, one teaspoon each soda and ginger, one tablespoon each cloves and nutmeg, two tablespoons cinnamon. One pint blackberry jam or molasses, two pounds almonds, one pound citron, one pound dates, one pound figs, three pounds raisins, and one cup fruit juice, or brandy if you use it. The day before baking prepare the fruit, shell and blanch the almonds. The next morning beat the butter and sugar to a cream, add yolks of eggs beaten light. Then stir the soda into the molasses or jam and add next, then add the flour and spices sifted together and the fruit juice or brandy. Dredge the fruit well with flour, add to the mixture, then the almonds, and fold in last the whites of eggs beaten to a stiff froth. Line the pan with heavy well-greased paper. Have the citron sliced very thin, put a layer of cake batter, then a layer of citron, alternately until all is used. This cake fills a pan ten inches in diameter and five inches deep. It should be baked six or seven hours in a very moderate oven. This is a splendid cake and will keep for months. Half the quantities make a large cake. All Larkin material used except eggs.

ETHEL C. DUDDERAR, GILBERTS CREEK, KY.

Pennsylvania Fruit Cake

Cream two-thirds cup lard or butter, add one cup sugar, and two eggs; beat quite light, add one cup molasses. Sift three and one-half cups flour with one and one-half teaspoons soda, one teaspoon each of salt and cloves, two teaspoons cinnamon and one-half teaspoon nutmeg. Sift three times. Add the sifted flour gradually with one cup strong coffee. Add one cup each of currants and raisins. These quantities make two loaf cakes. Bake in very moderate oven forty-five or sixty minutes. The cake is better if kept five weeks before cutting. All Larkin materials used except eggs.

Mrs. Alice Pennay, Kingsley, Pa.

Mother's Fruit Cake

Stir one and one-half cups butter or three-fourths of a pound, with three cups brown sugar, until light and creamy. Add one-half a nutmeg grated, one teaspoon each cinnamon, cloves and mace. Dissolve one teaspoon soda in one-half cup sour cream, add to it one-half cup molasses and mix with the other ingredients. Add six eggs, beating each in separately. Sift four cups flour, add to cake mixture and one-half cup fruit juice, or brandy if you use it. Add one pound seeded raisins, one pound washed and dried currants, and one-half pound citron, orange and lemon peel mixed and shredded fine. Sprinkle the fruit with some of the flour and mix together well before adding to the cake. Beat or knead ten minutes then put into tins lined with greased paper. Place in moderate oven and bake slowly for three or four hours. These cakes improve with keeping.

Mrs. W. L. Laxton, Roanoke, Va.

Layer Cake

Cream one-half cup butter, add one cup sugar and mix very smooth. Sift two cups flour with two teaspoons baking powder and add to the sugar and butter alternately with one-half cup of milk mixed with two eggs beaten light. Add one-half teaspoon of any Larkin Flavoring Extract. Bake in layers and put together with any frosting desired.

Mrs. B. L. Tubman, Washington, D. C.

Kentucky Layer Cake

Cream one-half cup butter, add one cup sugar and two eggs; beat very light. Sift two cups flour with one-half teaspoon soda, add the flour and one-half cup of any home-made wine or Larkin Currant or Grape Jelly and one cup of seeded raisins. Bake in a square loaf or layer-cake pans. Good with or without icing.

Mrs. Albert Beaty, Oakville, Ky.

Quick Cream Cake without Shortening

Sift three times, one and one-half cups flour with one-half teaspoon salt, one and one-half teaspoons baking powder and one cup sugar. Break two eggs into measuring cup, fill with sweet cream, add to the flour mixture with one-half teaspoon flavoring extract. Beat three minutes. Bake in layers or a loaf. If sour cream, use one-half teaspoon soda instead of baking powder.

MRS. MARK J. MUDGETT, NORTH POMFRET, VT.

Cream Puffs

Put one cup water and one-third cup butter into a sauce-pan. When it boils stir in one cup flour all at once and stir until it leaves the edge of the sauce-pan. Let the mixture cool, then add three eggs, one at a time and beat each one in well before adding another. Mix until smooth, drop by the spoonful on a buttered pan a little distance apart to allow for spreading. Bake thirty minutes in hot oven or until well done. If in doubt as to the cakes being done, take one from the oven, if it does not shrivel up in a few minutes, they are done. This makes fifteen small puffs. When cold fill with cream filling prepared as follows:

One pint milk, four tablespoons corn starch, one teaspoon butter, three eggs, three-fourths cup sugar, one-fourth teaspoon salt, one-half teaspoon vanilla. Wet the corn starch with cold milk, scald the balance of the pint, add sugar and salt, cook five minutes. Beat the eggs, add two tablespoons of the corn starch mixture to them, then pour into the sauce-pan with the rest, and cook several minutes. Take from fire, add vanilla and butter. When cool fill the puffs and serve.

MRS. R. H. SINGER, NORTH BROOKFIELD, MASS.

Pound Cake

Cream one pound butter, add one pound white sugar, the yolks of nine eggs and beat until very light. Then add one pound flour (four cups) sifted with one teaspoon baking powder. Add one tablespoon lemon juice and one-half teaspoon mace if the flavor is liked. Beat the whites of eggs quite stiff, gradually add them with the flour. Bake in a large pan lined with waxed paper in a very moderate oven (see rules for baking).

If you wish a fruit cake add two teaspoons Larkin Allspice and a quarter pound each of Larkin Raisins, Currants, Dates and mixed peel. This cake is much better if kept several weeks before using.

MRS. W. S. SHIFLET, HARRISONBURG, VA.

Sponge Cake

Six eggs, one cup sugar, one tablespoon lemon juice, grated rind of one lemon, one cup flour, one-fourth teaspoon salt. Beat yolks until thick and lemon-colored, add sugar gradually and continue beating. Add rind and juice of lemon and the whites beaten stiff and dry. Beat with egg-beater until well blended. Remove beater and carefully cut and fold in the flour and salt sifted together. Do not stir this cake as it would take away the lightness. Bake fifty to sixty minutes in a slow oven. Invert pan while cake cools.

MISS BESSIE RENFREW, LENOX, MASS.

Four-Egg Sponge Cake

Four eggs, one cup sugar, four tablespoons cold water, one cup flour sifted with one teaspoon baking powder. One-half teaspoon flavoring extract. Beat yolks of eggs, add the sugar, then the cold water and the sifted flour, then the extract. Fold in the beaten whites of eggs. Bake in a moderate oven forty-five minutes.

MISS A. ROMMEL, ELIZABETH, N. J.

Molasses Layer Cake

One-half cup Larkin Lard, one and one-half cups Larkin Molasses, one egg, one-half cup thick cream (sweet or sour), three cups flour sifted three times with one teaspoon each of Larkin Soda and Baking Powder, and two teaspoons ginger. Cream the lard, add the molasses, the egg and sifted flour and milk. Beat briskly for two minutes. Put into three layer-cake pans or into a loaf-pan. Bake in a moderate oven.

DR. EDITH K. NEEL, SANTA ROSA, FLA.

Corn Starch Cake

Cream one cup butter, add two cups powdered sugar, one cup milk and one teaspoon flavoring extract. Sift together two cups flour, one cup corn starch, two teaspoons baking powder, one-half teaspoon salt. Fold in stiffly-beaten whites of six eggs. Place in a greased cake-pan. Bake in a moderate oven forty-five minutes. Cover with cocoanut icing.

MRS. ANDREW WILHELM, EASTON, PA.

Gold Cake

Cream one-half cup butter, add one cup sugar, mix thoroughly then add the yolks of four eggs. Sift two cups flour with two teaspoons of baking powder and one-half teaspoon salt. Add gradually to the butter and sugar with one-half cup milk and one-half teaspoon any Larkin Flavoring Extract desired. Bake in tube pan about thirty minutes in moderate oven.

MRS. G. REUBENS, PEARL RIVER, N. Y.

Father's Coffee Cake

Cook together for five minutes one cup sugar, one cup coffee, two tablespoons cocoa. While this is cooling, cream one-half cup butter, add one cup sugar, two eggs, then add one cup cold coffee. Sift together two cups flour, one teaspoon soda, one teaspoon baking powder and add to the other ingredients. Stir in the cool cooked mixture and bake in a loaf. The batter will not be very thick but do not add more flour. Cover with white icing.

MRS. J. L. COX, ANGUS, NEBR.

English Jam Cake

Cream three-fourths cup butter in a mixing bowl. Add one cup sugar and three eggs beaten in singly. Sift together two cups Larkin Pastry Flour, one teaspoon each Larkin Soda, Cinnamon and Nutmeg, sift three times, add one-half cup milk or water and one-half cup Larkin Raspberry Jam. Put into a long, narrow pan; bake in a very moderate oven forty-five minutes. This also makes an excellent dessert if cut in small rounds or squares and covered with whipped cream. Decorate with pecans or English walnuts.

MRS. ALBERT BEATY, OAKVILLE, KY.

Chocolate Cream Cakes

Beat one egg light in the mixing bowl, add one cup sugar and one cup cream, sweet or sour. Sift together one cup flour and five tablespoons Larkin Cocoa with one teaspoon Larkin Soda; add sufficient flour to thicken. Flavor with Larkin Vanilla Extract, bake in gem- or layer-cake pans twenty minutes. Serve hot or cold.

MRS. C. A. ENGLAND, VAN METER, IOWA.

Cocoa Tea Cakes

Cream one-third cup butter with one cup sugar. Beat in singly, three eggs, add one-half cup each of Larkin Corn Starch and flour sifted with one-fourth cup cocoa, one teaspoon baking powder and one-fourth teaspoon salt. Add one-half teaspoon vanilla or lemon extract. Put in muffin-pans and bake in moderate oven twenty minutes. Delicious. May also be baked in layers.

L. J. SIGMAN, WATER VALLEY, MISS.

Ice-Cream Cake

Make a good sponge cake, bake half an inch thick in layer-cake pans. When quite cold, take a pint of thick sweet cream, beat until it looks like ice-cream, sweeten and flavor with Larkin Vanilla. Blanch and chop one-half pound almonds, stir into cream and spread thickly between layers. This is the queen of all cakes.

MISS RUTH RIGGIN, CRISFIELD, MD.

Watermelon Cake

For the white part use four tablespoons butter, one-half cup sugar, one-third cup milk, one and one-half cups flour, one and one-half teaspoons baking powder, whites of two eggs beaten light and one-half teaspoon almond extract. For the pink part use the same quantities, taking two yolks of eggs and one-half teaspoon vanilla extract and sufficient Larkin Cherry-Red Culinary Paste to make a pretty pink color, add one-half cup raisins. Line a long narrow pan with waxed paper and pour the first mixture into it, and the pink over that. Bake as layer cake. When cool make a white icing and color it a pale green with Larkin Apple-Green Culinary Paste. Cut in strips to serve.

MRS. J. H. STOCKMANN, FREDRICKSBURG, VA.

Fourth-of-July Cake

Use the same recipe as given for watermelon cake, leaving out the raisins in pink part. For a third or blue part, use one-fourth cup butter, one-half cup sugar, one cup flour, one teaspoon baking powder and one egg. Use juice from canned blueberries or logan berries to mix. Put together with white icing, having red cake at the bottom, then white layer, and blue on top. Decorate with tiny flags.

LARKIN KITCHEN.

Potato Cake

Put into a Larkin Cake-Maker, two-thirds cup butter with two cups sugar and three eggs. Sift together two and one-half cups flour with one teaspoon ground cinnamon, half a teaspoon ground nutmeg, two teaspoons baking powder. Sift three times, add the flour and one cup hot mashed potato, two squares (or ounces) of Larkin Unsweetened Chocolate which has been melted over hot water, one-half cup milk, three yolks and two whites of eggs, one teaspoon Larkin Vanilla Extract and one cup of chopped walnuts. Stir for five minutes, put into a greased square cake-pan, bake in a moderate oven forty-five minutes. Delicious as a dessert with whipped cream.

MRS. CHAS. W. HAMILTON, EAST ST. LOUIS, ILL.

Milkless, Eggless, Butterless Cake

Boil together three minutes, one cup brown sugar, one cup water, one-third cup lard or cooking oil, one cup Larkin Seeded Raisins, one-half teaspoon nutmeg and one teaspoon cinnamon. When thoroughly cool, add two cups flour sifted with one-half teaspoon each of baking powder, soda and salt. Bake in a square pan in a moderate oven thirty-five minutes. One-half cup nut meats may be added if a richer cake is desired.

MRS. EDWIN W. FISHBURN, DENVER, COLO.

Chocolate Nut Cake

Put into a double-boiler, two ounces unsweetened chocolate, one-half cup brown sugar, one-half cup cold water and the yolk of one egg. Cook until thick, then add one teaspoon vanilla extract and one cup chopped nuts—pecans or walnuts. Set aside to cool. Cream two-thirds cup butter or other shortening, add one cup brown sugar and two eggs beaten light. Dissolve one teaspoon soda in one-half cup sour milk; add with two cups flour. Fold in chocolate mixture and bake in loaf or layers. Cover with white frosting.

MARY KELLY, KILBOURN, WIS.

Rich Chocolate Cake

Cream one cup butter, add two cups sugar and mix quite smooth. Add the beaten yolks of five eggs, one cup sour milk, one teaspoon soda dissolved in a tablespoon of hot water and one-half cake or four ounces Larkin Chocolate melted over hot water. Stir all together then add two and one-half cups flour. Fold in last the stiffly-beaten whites of two eggs. Bake in layers or a long shallow pan. If a layer cake, cut up Larkin Marshmallows in small pieces and put between the two cakes while still hot. Cover with white frosting. This will keep a week.

M. C. TOPPAN, HAMPTON, N. H.

New Orleans Cakes

One cup Larkin Molasses, two cups Larkin Light Yellow Sugar, one-half cup softened lard, one teaspoon Larkin Soda, one teaspoon salt, one teaspoon ginger, two teaspoons cinnamon and one cup hot water. Use enough flour to make a soft cake or hard gingerbread, or use more flour and make drop or rolled-out cookies. You can stir this up and bake a cake for tea (make the consistency of layer cake). Then the next day add more flour to what was left and bake a pan of dropped cookies or make a steamed pudding and serve with sweet sauce.

MRS. A. J. SKELLIE, LITTLE ROCK, ARK.

Pork Cake

Put one pound fat salt pork through Larkin Food-Chopper, pour over pork two cups boiling coffee or water. Put one pound Larkin Raisins and one-fourth pound citron peel through food-chopper using coarse knife, add to pork with one cup currants, two cups brown sugar. Stir one teaspoon soda into one cup molasses. Sift six cups flour with two teaspoons each of cloves and cinnamon and one teaspoon salt. Add one more cup flour if necessary. Bake in four loaves in one-pound bread-pans. If wrapped in waxed paper and put into stone jar, it will keep for months.

MRS. LEROY STEPHENSON, MADISON, WIS.

Apple Sauce Birthday Cake

Put through the food-chopper (using coarse knife), one-fourth pound each of citron, candied lemon and orange peel, also one pound raisins. Sift together, four cups flour, two teaspoons each nutmeg, cinnamon and cloves, and one teaspoon each of soda and salt. Cream together, one cup butter and two cups brown sugar. Add all ingredients with two and one-half cups unsweetened apple sauce. Line cake-pan with waxed paper and bake in slow oven for one and one-quarter hours. Will keep fresh six weeks or more if tightly covered.

MRS. W. WAIBEL, SYRACUSE, N. Y.

Eggless Apple Sauce Cake

Cream one-half cup butter or other shortening, add one cup brown sugar. Sift one and one-half cups flour with one teaspoon each of soda, salt, cinnamon, cloves and cocoa. Mix with one cup unsweetened apple sauce; bake in moderate oven forty-five minutes. One cup of raisins may be added to this.

MRS. HARRY BUNN, SCHENECTADY, N. Y.

Spice Cake

Cream one cup lard, add one cup each of sugar, molasses and thick sour milk, four cups flour sifted three times with two teaspoons soda and one teaspoon each cinnamon and nutmeg. Add two teaspoons vinegar, bake in square pan in moderate oven thirty-five minutes. Ice with caramel or white frosting.

MRS. J. E. BLAKE, MARBLE ROCK, IOWA.

Rich Spice Cakes

Two cups brown sugar, one cup lard and butter mixed, three eggs, one cup sour milk. Sift three and one-half cups flour with one teaspoon each Larkin Salt, Soda, Cinnamon, Nutmeg, Allspice and Cloves. Add one pound chopped raisins and one-half pound walnut meats. Take a spoonful of the mixture, roll in sugar, place on pans one inch apart, raise twenty minutes and bake. This may be baked in a loaf and will keep moist for weeks. Wrap in waxed paper before putting away.

MRS. IDA FETTERMAN, PUNXSUTAWNEY, PA.

French Pastry

Cut a sheet of sponge cake into small rounds; dip in chocolate frosting. While this is still moist lay split blanched almonds cut in halves around each little cake like daisy petals. In the center drop the daisy heart made of fondant, colored yellow. Or you may use white fondant and split almonds which have been delicately browned in the oven, making the marguerite heart of chocolate.

MRS. JOHN HAUSER, ROCHESTER, N. Y.

Angel Food

Whites of eight eggs, one teaspoon cream of tartar, one cup sugar, three-fourths cup Larkin Pastry Flour, one-fourth teaspoon salt, three-fourths teaspoon vanilla. Beat egg whites until frothy, add cream of tartar and beat until they are stiff; add sugar gradually. Mix flour and salt and sift four times, fold into the eggs and sugar and add vanilla. Bake in an unbuttered tube pan forty to fifty minutes.

MRS. ALBERT CARPENTER, GULDERLAND, N. Y.

Cocoa Angel Cake

Beat whites of five eggs until foamy, add one-half teaspoon cream of tartar and beat until dry. Sift together, one cup sugar and one-fourth cup cocoa with one-half cup Larkin Pastry Flour. Fold into eggs and flavor with one-half teaspoon vanilla. Bake one-half hour in a tube pan. When cold cover with a thin boiled icing.

MRS. JOHN DENKER, LAKEFIELD, MINN.

Cocoanut Macaroons

Beat the whites of three eggs until stiff, gradually add one-half pound Larkin Powdered Sugar (or one and one-fourth cups), one-half package Larkin Cocoanut, one-half teaspoon Larkin Almond Extract. Mix gently together, drop from a teaspoon about one inch apart on Larkin Waxed Paper. Bake in a moderate oven about twenty minutes. When cool brush the under side of paper with water and remove cakes. This recipe makes three dozen delicious macaroons.

MRS. G. A. RANDALL, PROVIDENCE, R. I.

Marguerites

Beat the whites of three eggs until stiff; add gradually six tablespoons powdered sugar, one-half teaspoon Larkin Vanilla and five tablespoons chopped nuts. Drop with a teaspoon on buttered pans; bake in moderate oven until golden brown or spread over Larkin Saltines and brown lightly in a slow oven.

MARY E. RAYMOND, WAYNE, MICH.

Cocoanut Marguerites

Boil one cup sugar with one-half cup water until it spins a thread, drop in six marshmallows cut in small pieces. Pour the mixture gradually upon the whites of two eggs which have been beaten dry, add one-half cup cocoanut and when cool, one-half teaspoon vanilla and one-half cup chopped nut meats. Tint with Larkin Cherry-Red Culinary Paste, spread on crackers and bake in moderate oven until slightly brown. Very pretty for a luncheon.

MRS. WM. MCALPIN, JAMESTOWN, N. Y.

Jelly Roll

Beat three eggs very light. Add one cup of sugar gradually. Sift one cup flour with one teaspoon baking powder and one-fourth teaspoon salt, add two tablespoons milk and mix lightly but thoroughly. Line the bottom and sides of pan with waxed paper. Cover bottom of pan with mixture and spread evenly. Bake twelve minutes in a moderate oven. Take from oven and turn onto a paper sprinkled with powdered sugar. Quickly remove paper and cut off a thin strip from sides and ends of cake. Spread with jelly or jam which has been beaten to consistency to spread easily, then roll. After cake has been rolled, roll waxed paper around it to keep it in shape. The work must be done quickly, or cake will crack in rolling.

MRS. R. HELM, MT. VERNON, ILL.

Madeira Cake

Cream one cup butter, add two and one-half cups sugar, yolks of three eggs; beat quite light. Sift four cups flour with one-half teaspoon soda, add the grated rinds of two lemons. Take care not to grate any of the white pith, only the yellow rind should be used. Add the strained juice of the lemons and two-thirds cup of milk, or water. Fold in the stiffly-beaten egg whites. Bake in a large round cake-pan in a medium oven, one hour. When cake has baked twenty minutes put two long thin slices of citron peel across the top.

MRS. C. P. DEANE, ALBERENE, VA.

Rich Blackberry Cake

One cup butter, two cups sugar, five eggs. Sift together three times, four cups flour, one teaspoon soda, two teaspoons each of baking powder and cinnamon, one teaspoon allspice, one-half teaspoon nutmeg. Cream the butter, add the sugar; beat in one egg at a time until you have three, then add some sifted flour and more eggs until you have five. Add the flour, one cup of thick sour milk, and one cup canned blackberries or blackberry jam. Bake in round cake-pans with a funnel or in small bread-pans for forty-five minutes. See directions for baking fruit cake. This cake tastes the best when kept five weeks before being cut.

MISS ADA C. MITZEL, BETHANY, OHIO.

Crumb Cake

Two and one-half cups flour, one and one-half cups brown sugar, one-half cup butter. Mix together the same as pie-crust. Take out one cup crumbs, then add one cup sour milk, and one teaspoon soda. Put in greased meat-pan, sprinkle the crumbs over the top and bake in a moderate oven.

MRS. JOHN BRADY, KENT, OHIO.

FROSTINGS AND FILLINGS

Chocolate Filling No. 1

One-half cake Larkin Unsweetened Chocolate, one-half cup sweet cream, one and one-half cups granulated sugar. Boil together about five minutes. Beat until cool. Then add one teaspoon Larkin Vanilla Extract, spread thickly between layers and on top.

MRS. C. C. LYONS, HALE, MO.

Chocolate Filling No. 2

Take one-half package of Larkin Prepared Chocolate Pudding and make according to directions with two cups of milk. Put between and on top of layer cake. Cover with whipped cream or plain white frosting. This is delicious and inexpensive and makes a large cake.

MRS. M. AMOROSA, ROCKLAND, MASS.

Chocolate Frosting

Melt one and one-half ounces Larkin Unsweetened Chocolate over hot water. Then add one-fourth cup scalded cream, a pinch of Larkin Salt, one egg yolk, one tablespoon butter, one-half teaspoon Larkin Vanilla. Stir in powdered sugar to make right consistency to spread. A pleasant change when whipping cream for cake is to put in two dessert-spoons of Larkin Cocoa before you begin to whip. Add sugar and vanilla and you have a delicious frosting.

MRS. C. G. PENNIMAN, BROOKLYN, N. Y.

Fruit Filling

One-half cup mashed strawberries (raspberries or peaches may be used), one cup powdered sugar, white of one egg. Put all together and beat briskly until stiff enough to stay on layer cake.

MRS. FRANK S. MERRILL, BRISTOL, CONN.

Rich Cocoanut Frosting

Take two cups whipped cream, two cups Larkin Cocoanut, juice of one orange or one teaspoon Larkin Lemon or Orange Extract, one-half cup powdered sugar. Mix lightly but thoroughly; spread between and on cake.

MRS. JAMES A. TENEYCK, PLUCKEMIN, N. J.

Minnehaha Filling

Chop one cup raisins, one cup English walnuts; add one cup grated cocoanut; mix together; boil one cup granulated sugar and six tablespoons water until it threads; pour while hot over the fruit and nuts. Spread between layers; put cocoanut on top of cake.

HATTIE OSBORN, BORING, MD.

Mocha Frosting

One cup powdered sugar, three tablespoons butter, one tablespoon milk, one tablespoon strong coffee, one-fourth teaspoon vanilla extract. Mix well with spoon, then beat light with silver fork.

MRS. FRED W. GURNEY, NORTH ATTLEBORO, MASS.

Lemon Filling

Put three-fourths cup Larkin Granulated Sugar, one tablespoon cold water, one beaten egg, juice and grated rind of one lemon into a double sauce-pan. Stir until it thickens. Delicious.

MRS. JAMES A. SIPES, DETROIT, MICH.

Lemon Icing

Put one and one-half tablespoons butter into a basin, melt over hot water, add one tablespoon cream or evaporated milk, one-half teaspoon lemon extract and sufficient powdered sugar to spread.

MRS. W. N. POPPE, BROOKLYN, N. Y.

Boiled Icing

Put one cup of Larkin Granulated Sugar with one-fourth cup of water; add a pinch of cream of tartar. Stir until the sugar is dissolved; then let it boil until, when tried with a fork, the syrup will end in a fine thread-like stream. Remove immediately from the fire and pour slowly over the stiffly-beaten whites of two eggs. Add one-half teaspoon of any Larkin Extract. Beat until the icing is cool; spread at once.

MRS. BENJAMIN H. MILLER, COLUMBIA CITY, IND.

Raisin Filling

Take one-half package Larkin Raisins and stew until tender; cool and drain off the water. Mash with a potato masher (do not chop them), add two-thirds cup powdered sugar and one-third box Larkin Shredded Cocoanut. If this is a little dry add a very little milk, spread between and on top of cake. It is delicious. This is enough for a three-layer cake.

MRS. CLYDE CROMAN, MARION, OHIO.

Marshmallow Filling and Frosting

Take one-half pound marshmallows; reserve sufficient whole marshmallows for top of cake; cut remainder into small pieces. Cook one and one-half cups sugar with one-third cup water until it hairs. Have ready two whites of eggs whipped to a froth; add the syrup; then put in cut marshmallows. Spread upon both layers of cake. Put a little hot water into bowl, dip one side of marshmallow and put on top layer of cake as quickly as possible.

MRS. WALTER R. HERBERT, BEDFORD, IOWA.

Mock Marshmallow Frosting

Soften two tablespoons Larkin Gelatine in six tablespoons cold water. Put over hot water to melt. Boil two cups Larkin Granulated Sugar with one-half cup water until it will thread, pour into the gelatine, flavor with Larkin Vanilla Extract and beat until thick and white. Nuts are a fine addition.

FLORENCE E. TITUS, BRATTLEBORO, VT.

Caramel Frosting

One cup brown sugar, one-fourth cup boiling water, white of one egg. Take one-fourth of the sugar and put into a small sauce-pan and brown over the fire. Then add the boiling water and the rest of the sugar. Boil until it falls in a heavy thread from the spoon. Pour it slowly onto the beaten white of one egg, beating all the time. Beat until it is cool and thick; spread between layers and on top of cake.

MRS. WILLIAM CONNELLY, FALL RIVER, MASS.

Melba Cake Filling

Boil together for five minutes, one cup milk, one and one-half pounds Larkin Brown Sugar and one jar Larkin Peanut Butter. Then add one-fourth cup each of walnuts, almonds and hazelnuts coarsely chopped, to the boiling syrup, beat until thick, put in jelly glasses and seal up. This will keep a long while. When ready to use add whipped cream to spread.

MRS. P. COLEMAN, CASTLETON, KANS.

Cream Frosting

Beat whites of two eggs until light but not stiff, add gradually five tablespoons of granulated sugar. Put over hot water and steam ten minutes. Flavor with Larkin Vanilla. Beat until cold. This is almost like whipped cream.

MRS. F. J. TERPENNING, NEWARK VALLEY, N. Y.

Orange Icing

Strain the juice of two oranges—add enough Larkin Powdered Sugar to spread easily. Color with Larkin Yellow Culinary Paste and flavor delicately with Larkin Lemon Extract. This is delicious and quite a help during the hot summer months, when you don't care to cook icings.

MRS. HENRY DAVIS, NEW DECATUR, ALA.

Hot Water Frosting

Put two tablespoons boiling water into a bowl; add powdered sugar and three tablespoons Larkin Cocoa to make it the right consistency to spread; add one teaspoon melted butter; flavor with Larkin Vanilla.

MRS. CARRIE K. BAKER, BREWER, MAINE.

Maple Icing

Moisten one cup powdered sugar, with strong coffee so that it will spread. Flavor with one teaspoon of Larkin Maple Flavor Imitation Extract. This makes a delicious and quick icing.

MRS. FRANK BONINIE, MONESSEN, PA.

Vinegar Frosting

One cup brown sugar, one cup white sugar, ten tablespoons water, two tablespoons vinegar, cream of tartar the size of a pea; boil all together until a little dropped into cold water can be gathered into a ball; pour slowly over the well-beaten white of one egg; beat until stiff. Flavor with one teaspoon Larkin Vanilla Extract. This icing never gets hard. Spread between the layers of cake and on top.

MRS. R. V. BUCKAGE, VINCENTOWN, N. J.

Fig Filling

Chop three-fourths pound of Larkin Sun-Dried Figs; add three-fourths cup Larkin Sugar, juice of one-half lemon; stew together until soft and smooth, and spread between layers.

MRS. EVERETT B. CURTIS, NORTH BEND, OREGON.

Pineapple Filling

Empty a can of shredded pineapple into sauce-pan and bring to a boil; thicken with two tablespoons Larkin Corn Starch, boil a few minutes and let cool; then spread between the layers. A chocolate frosting is excellent on this cake.

MRS. A. J. LAWALL, NEWARK, N. J.

Hot Water Gingerbread

Mix together one cup molasses, one-half cup sugar, one-third cup butter or lard. Sift two and one-half cups flour with two teaspoons soda, one tablespoon ginger, one-half teaspoon each cloves and cinnamon, one-half teaspoon salt. Stir together well with one cup boiling water, hastily stir in two well-beaten eggs. This is very thin but do not add more flour. May be baked in gem-pans, or layers. If Larkin Waxed Paper is cut to fit the bottom of the cake tins after they are greased, the cake will not stick. As this is a very soft cake, let it cool before removing from pans. Cover with plain white frosting. Will remain moist two weeks.

Mrs. Elmer H. Crisler, Clyde, N. Y.

Sour Milk Gingerbread

Mix one-fourth cup Larkin Cooking Oil or Lard with one cup sugar and one egg. Beat very light. Add one-half cup molasses. Sift two teaspoons Larkin Ginger, one teaspoon Larkin Cinnamon, one-fourth teaspoon salt, and one-half teaspoon soda with one and three-fourths cups flour. Add flour alternately with one-half cup sour milk. Pour into greased pans and bake in moderate oven thirty to forty minutes.

Mrs. J. Scanlon, Buffalo, N. Y.

Eggless Gingerbread

Cream one-half cup butter or lard, with one cup brown sugar, add one-half cup milk. Sift together two cups flour, two teaspoons baking powder, and one and one-half teaspoons ginger. Add to the first mixture with one-half cup milk. Spread thinly with a spatula on a buttered baking sheet. Bake in a moderate oven twenty minutes. Cut in squares immediately after removing from oven. Serve cold or warm with coffee.

Mrs. F. Richardson, Santa Rosa, Fla.

To Cut Cookies

When making Ginger Snaps, Cookies, etc., if the dough is shaped in long narrow rolls and chilled on ice or left in a cold place over night it may be sliced off instead of rolling. This saves a good deal of time and is very satisfactory.

Miss Annie E. Graybill, Buchanan, Va.

Soft Molasses Cookies

Cream one and one-half cups brown sugar and one cup lard. Add two eggs and one cup molasses, beat well. Sift together five cups bread flour, one teaspoon soda, one tablespoon ground ginger, one teaspoon salt, add to other ingredients. Now add one cup boiling water very gradually and beat well. Drop by the spoonful onto greased baking sheets and bake in hot oven.

MRS. W. ED. HUGHES, EAST ROCHESTER, N. Y.

Boston Cookies

One cup butter, one and one-half cups Larkin Sugar, three eggs, one teaspoon Larkin Soda, one and one-half teaspoons hot water, three and one-fourth cups Larkin Bread Flour, one-half teaspoon salt, one teaspoon Larkin Cinnamon, one cup chopped walnuts, one-half cup each of Larkin Currants and Raisins, seeded and chopped. Cream the butter, add the sugar gradually, then the eggs, lightly beaten. Sift flour three times with salt, cinnamon and soda, then add nut meats, fruit and flour. Drop on greased pans with a teaspoon an inch apart. Bake in moderate oven. These will improve with keeping.

MRS. CHARLES J. PRANKARD, UPPER TROY, N. Y.

Jelly Cookies

One-half cup butter, one cup sugar, one egg, one-fourth cup sour milk, one-half teaspoon soda. Add flour enough to roll out thin. Cut in two layers. Use doughnut-cutter for top layer. Spread apple jelly or fig paste between. Bake in hot oven.

MATTIE E. ROBINSON, WILLIAMSTOWN, VT.

Spice Cookies

One cup molasses, one-half cup sugar, one-half cup each lard and butter, four cups flour, one teaspoon each ginger, salt, soda and cinnamon, one-half teaspoon nutmeg, two eggs. Heat molasses to boiling point, add sugar and shortening. Mix and sift dry ingredients, add to first mixture with the eggs lightly beaten. Chill and roll out. In warm weather prepare the mixture over night or some hours before using so that it may be easily rolled.

MRS. ANNA HOCKING, DUBUQUE, IOWA.

Graham Cookies

One egg, one cup brown sugar, one cup sour milk, one tablespoon molasses, four tablespoons shortening, one teaspoon each soda and cinnamon, two cups graham flour, one cup raisins. Drop on greased pans. These are delicious with or without raisins.

MRS. WALTER NICHOLS, BIRMINGHAM, MICH.

Oatmeal Cookies No. 1

Cream together one cup butter and Larkin Pure Lard mixed, add one cup Larkin Granulated Sugar. Sift together three cups Larkin Fancy Patent Flour, one teaspoon Larkin Soda and one teaspoon Larkin Cinnamon. Sift three times. Now add two cups Larkin Rolled Oats and one cup Larkin Seeded Raisins. Mix thoroughly. Beat light two eggs, add one tablespoon Larkin Evaporated Milk and five of water. Drop by the spoonful onto a greased baking sheet. Bake in a hot oven.

Mrs. L. Leslie Jones, Mansfield, Mass.

Rich Oatmeal Cookies No. 2

Three-fourths cup shortening, one cup sugar, two eggs. Sift two cups flour with one teaspoon each soda and cinnamon, three times, add two cups oatmeal, two cups chopped raisins, one cup chopped pecan or walnut meats, one cup Larkin Cocoanut, four tablespoons sour milk. Mix in order given, drop on buttered baking sheet, bake in medium oven.

Mrs. A. H. Cameron, San Antonio, Texas.

Christmas Cookies

One-fourth cup butter, one cup sugar, two eggs, one cup molasses, one cup sour cream, two teaspoons soda, one-fourth pound mixed candied peel, one-fourth pound almonds, one teaspoon cinnamon, one-half teaspoon nutmeg. Add sufficient flour to roll out, cut with fancy cutters, bake in moderate oven. These improve with keeping.

Mrs. Volney G. Pitcher, Jackson, Mich.

Hermits

Two cups brown sugar, three-fourths cup butter, two eggs well beaten, one teaspoon soda put into one-half cup boiling water, three cups flour, one cup chopped raisins and one cup currants. Cream the butter, add sugar, then add the well-beaten eggs and stir until well mixed; add the remaining ingredients. Drop on baking sheets, bake in a moderate oven.

Mrs. Jno. Marasek, Minneapolis, Minn.

Eggless Cookies

Sift together six cups flour, two teaspoons baking powder, one teaspoon salt, one teaspoon soda, one teaspoon nutmeg. Into this rub one cup shortening. Add two cups brown sugar and enough sour milk to make a soft dough. Roll out lightly, sprinkle with sugar and bake quickly. Raisins may be placed on some and jelly on others. Sweet milk may be used in place of sour.

Mrs. Luther Miller, New Philadelphia, Ohio.

Eggless Date Cookies

One cup sugar, one-half cup butter and lard mixed, one-half cup sour milk, two cups Larkin Rolled Oats put through food-chopper, one teaspoon soda, flour to make stiff enough to roll every thin. Mix in the usual manner, cut in any desired shape, and put together in pairs with the following filling:

Wash and remove stones from one-half pound Larkin Dates, add three-fourths cup sugar and one cup cold water. Cook twenty minutes, use when quite cold.

Mrs. Besse Binnall, Dow City, Iowa.

Special Peanut Cookies

Put three tablespoons Larkin Peanut Butter, one teaspoon lard, one and one-half cups granulated sugar, and two eggs into a mixing bowl. Stir and beat until mixture is quite light. Add two and one-half cups sifted flour and one teaspoon soda dissolved in three tablespoons thick sour milk. Flavor with one teaspoon Larkin Vanilla Extract. Roll and bake in a quick oven. This amount makes fifty cookies.

Mrs. G. W. Parrins, Lyons, N. Y.

Chocolate Cookies

Cream one-half cup butter, add one cup brown sugar, one egg, one-half cup sour milk, two squares or ounces Larkin Chocolate melted over hot water. Sift one and one-half cups flour with one-half teaspoon soda, add one-half cup raisins, one-half cup chopped walnut meats. Mix well and drop with a teaspoon on buttered pans or use more flour and roll out. Bake in a moderate oven. Nuts may be left out if not on hand.

Mrs. W. L. Austin, Alliance, Nebr.

Cocoanut or Sugar Cookies

Mix together thoroughly, one cup lard or butter, two cups sugar, two eggs, one cup cocoanut. Sift two and one-half cups flour with two teaspoons baking powder. If not stiff enough, add more flour to roll out quite thin. Bake quickly. All materials are Larkin except the eggs. For sugar cookies leave out cocoanut, add one teaspoon lemon extract.

Mrs. W. C. Hudson, Orangeburgh, N. Y.

Raisin Drop Cookies

Mix and beat well together, one and one-half cups brown sugar, two-thirds cup butter, three eggs. Add one and one-half cups raisins chopped fine, two and one-half cups flour, sifted with one teaspoon soda, one teaspoon cloves and nutmeg mixed. Drop on a baking sheet. Bake in slow oven.

Mrs. Ray F. Cossentine, Susquehanna, Pa.

Doughnuts

One cup sugar, one cup milk, two eggs beaten fine as silk,
A little nutmeg (lemon will do), of baking powder, teaspoons two,
Lightly stir the flour in, roll on pie-board not too thin;
Cut in diamonds, twists or rings, then drop with care the doughy things
Into fat that briskly swells, evenly the spongy cells.
Roll in sugar, lay to cool. Always use this simple rule.

For chocolate doughnuts use the above rule, add four tablespoons of cocoa with the flour, or two ounces of melted chocolate.

MRS. BELLE THORP OCKER, WEST UNION, IOWA.

Potato Doughnuts

Three tablespoons lard, three-fourths cup sugar, two eggs, one cup freshly mashed potato, one-fourth cup milk, sift together two and one-half cups flour, three teaspoons baking powder, one-half teaspoon salt, one-half teaspoon cinnamon, one-fourth teaspoon ground nutmeg. Cream the lard, add the sugar, then the eggs. Stir in the potato and milk. Add the flour gradually and use more if necessary. Roll and cut all the doughnuts before commencing the frying. Fry in deep lard or cooking oil. This rule will make three dozen. One cup of beef-suet melted with lard is good for frying.

RUTH WIGGINS, SHELBY, OHIO.

Buttermilk Doughnuts

Beat one egg, add one cup brown sugar and one cup buttermilk, two tablespoons butter or lard. Sift together four and one-half cups flour, one-half teaspoon Larkin Soda, one teaspoon Larkin Baking Powder, one-half teaspoon salt. Stir together. roll out. Cut, and fry in deep fat.

DESSIE L. NUZUM, WATSON, W. VA.

Baked Apple Pudding

Half fill a pudding dish with sliced apples, add sugar and spice, cook until almost soft. Set aside to cool. While still steaming cover with a batter made by sifting together one pint flour, two teaspoons baking powder, one-half teaspoon salt, and one-half cup sugar. Add one egg well beaten, two tablespoons melted shortening and three-fourths cup milk. Bake in a moderate oven one-half hour. Any dried fruit may be used instead of apples. Serve with a sweet sauce or cream.

MARY G. MURPHY, ROXBURY, MASS.

Spiced Apple Pudding

Sift together two cups flour, one teaspoon allspice, one-half teaspoon ground nutmeg and two teaspoons baking powder. Add one beaten egg, one cup sugar, four tablespoons soft butter, one cup milk and one cup cooked Larkin Canned Apples. Mix well and spread in a flat pan. Bake forty-five minutes in a moderate oven or steam one and one-half hours in a covered bowl. Serve with sweet sauce.

H. HARPER, PORTSMOUTH, VA.

Suet Pudding

Take two cups flour, two eggs, two cups raisins, one cup currants, one-half teaspoon salt, one-half cup chopped suet, one-half cup sour milk, one teaspoon soda. Stir all together and put into food pan of Larkin Double-Boiler. Steam three hours. Serve with sweet sauce.

MRS. E. GRINDROD, CONNELLSVILLE, PA.

Queen Pudding

One pint bread-crumbs, two tablespoons melted butter, one cup sugar, one quart milk, three eggs, one teaspoon lemon extract. Soak the crumbs in the milk for half hour; beat yolks of eggs with the sugar until yellow, add the lemon extract and butter. Pour into baking-dish and bake for one-half hour. When done, spread a layer of jelly or jam over the top. Beat the egg whites quite stiff; add four tablespoons granulated sugar and spread over the pudding. Brown lightly in a moderate oven and serve.

MRS. ALBRECHT, JAMAICA, N. Y.

Marshmallow Pudding

Soften one-half package Larkin Gelatine in one-half cup cold water. Add one cup sugar to one cup boiling water; when sugar is dissolved add gelatine. Beat the whites of four eggs very stiff and pour the liquid over them beating all the time as for boiled icing. Take one-third of the mixture and color with Larkin Apple-Green Culinary Paste, add to it one-fourth cup each of chopped pineapple, Maraschino cherries and English walnuts. Pour one-half of the white mixture into an oblong pan, then the pink and the white last; stand aside to cool. Cut in slices like brick ice-cream. Serve with a custard made with yolks of two eggs, one pint milk, one-half cup sugar, and one teaspoon corn starch. Flavor with vanilla.

Mrs. J. Herbert Robinson, Washington, D. C.

Sea-Foam Pudding

Scald three cups milk; dilute three tablespoons Larkin Corn Starch in one-fourth cup milk. Add a little of the scalded milk to the corn starch; pour back into sauce-pan; add one-half cup sugar and cook five minutes. Remove from fire; add one-half teaspoon extract and the stiffly-beaten whites of two eggs. Pour into mold. Serve with cream or boiled custard.

Mrs. Louise M. Cobb, South Boston, Mass.

Larkin Cocoanut Pudding

One pint milk; one-half cup Larkin Sugar; one-half cup rolled crackers; two tablespoons Larkin Shredded Cocoanut; pinch of Larkin Salt; yolks of two eggs; one teaspoon Larkin Lemon Flavoring Extract. Bake like custard. Beat whites of eggs, add a little sugar, put on top and brown in oven.

Mrs. E. A. Whitney, Melrose, Mass.

Steamed Chocolate Pudding

Melt two ounces chocolate over hot water; beat one egg light, add one cup milk, sift three teaspoons baking powder with two cups of flour and one-fourth teaspoon salt. Add egg and milk gradually to flour, adding chocolate last. Pour into buttered mold; steam one and one-half hours. Serve with creamy sauce.

Mrs. R. E. Smith, Milan, Pa.

Inexpensive Plum Pudding

Mix thoroughly two cups stale bread-crumbs, one cup Larkin Molasses, one cup sweet milk, one-half cup or one-fourth pound chopped suet, one egg, one teaspoon Larkin Cinnamon, one-half teaspoon Larkin Ground Cloves and Nutmeg, one cup raisins mixed with one-half cup flour and one-fourth teaspoon Larkin Soda. Put into a tin can or pail. Steam four hours. Serve with sweet sauce.

Mrs. James F. Ripley, Bethel, Vt.

Old English Plum Pudding

Put into a mixing bowl one cup suet chopped fine, grate one raw carrot and one potato, add one cup sugar, three-fourths cup molasses, three eggs, one teaspoon salt, two cups Larkin Raisins, one cup currants, one cup sour milk, one teaspoon soda; add sufficient flour to the mixture to make a stiff batter. Steam four hours in a covered bowl. Serve with sweet or hard sauce.

Miss Alice E. Seidmore, Ballston Spa, N. Y.

Thanksgiving Pudding

Three and one-half cups milk, eighteen crackers rolled fine, one cup sugar, four eggs, one teaspoon each allspice and salt, one-half pound seeded raisins, one-half cup butter. Pour milk over crackers. Leave twenty minutes. Add sugar, eggs slightly beaten, allspice, salt and butter. Parboil raisins until soft, add to mixture, turn into buttered pudding dish, bake slowly two and one-half hours. Stir once to prevent raisins settling. Serve with sweet sauce.

Mrs. George Balcom, Natick, Mass.

Date and Nut Pudding

One and one-half cups flour, two teaspoons baking powder, one cup sugar, two eggs, one cup each of chopped dates and walnuts. Mix as a cake. Put dates and walnuts through a Larkin Food-Chopper and add last. This may be spread in pie-pans and baked one-half hour in a moderate oven, but I prefer to put it into small cups and steam three-fourths of an hour in a Larkin Steam Cooker. Will serve six people. Serve with whipped cream.

Mrs. P. H. Overgard, Albert Lea, Minn.

Stale Cake Pudding

If you have any stale spice or fruit cake on hand, break it up in small pieces. Use half as much milk as you have cake. Mix together. Put into bowl and steam one hour. Sometimes a stale cake may be bought for a few cents at the baker's. It will make a good, cheap pudding. Serve with hard or sweet sauce.

E. L. Gibbs, Campello, Mass.

Cranberry Pudding

One-third cup butter, one cup sugar, two eggs, one-half cup milk, one and one-half cups flour, one and one-half teaspoons baking powder, one cup raw cranberries, one-half teaspoon lemon extract. Mix as for layer cake. Add cranberries and flavoring extract last. Bake in medium oven. Serve warm with hard or sweet sauce.

Miss Orril Newland, Hoopeston, Ill.

Baked Rhubarb Pudding

Wash fresh rhubarb. Do not remove the skin, cut in one-inch pieces until you have four cups. Put into a pudding dish with four or five slices of buttered bread cut in cubes and one cup sugar. Bake twenty minutes in moderate oven. Cover the pudding during the first ten minutes and then you will need no water as the rhubarb is juicy.

MISS JESSIE M. WILL, CANAL WINCHESTER, OHIO.

Graham Pudding

Two and one-half cups graham flour, one cup milk (or Larkin Evaporated Milk diluted with water), one cup molasses, one teaspoon soda, one cup currants or raisins, a pinch of salt. Mix all together, steam in double-boiler for two hours. It is good served with lemon sauce but best with whipped cream. This pudding is what everyone likes. It is almost as light as a soufflé and simply delicious. All Larkin material used.

MRS. WILLIAM REAHR, BUFFALO, N. Y.

Snow Pudding

Soak one-half package Larkin Gelatine in one-half cup cold water, dissolve in two cups boiling water, add two cups sugar, one-fourth cup lemon juice. Set aside in cool place; stir occasionally and when quite thick beat with whisk until frothy. Fold in whites of four eggs beaten quite stiff. When stiff enough to hold its shape, pile in glass dish. Serve with boiled custard.

MRS. CHARLES A. MARTIN, GARDNER, MASS.

Baked Caramel Pudding

Scald one quart milk, brown one-half cup Larkin Sugar in spider. Add milk to sugar and place on back of stove until sugar melts in the milk. Add two cups bread-crumbs, two beaten eggs, two-thirds cup sugar, one teaspoon Larkin Vanilla, one-fourth teaspoon Larkin Salt. Pour into buttered dish. Bake one hour in slow oven.

MRS. CHARLES P. LORING, AUBURN, MAINE.

Creamy Rice Pudding

To one quart new milk add four tablespoons Larkin Rice washed in cold water. Add three tablespoons sugar and a pinch of salt. Flavor with Larkin Nutmeg. Stir all together, place in a moderate oven and bake two hours. Stir once during the first hour. One and one-half cups raisins may be added if liked. They are not necessary however.

MRS. JOSEPH CLISH, MARQUETTE, MICH.

Rice Pudding in Double-Boiler

Put one-half cup Larkin Comet Rice into double-boiler with two cups sweet milk. Cook until quite soft. Add one-fourth cup Larkin Raisins and one-fourth teaspoon nutmeg. Cook twenty minutes. Then add one egg beaten with one-half cup sugar. Cook three minutes. Serve hot or cold.

MRS. CHARLES E. WILEY, NORTH AMHERST, MASS.

Baked Tapioca Pudding

Wash and soak three-fourths cup tapioca in two cups milk over night or for several hours. When ready to bake add another two cups milk, one-third cup sugar, one pinch salt and one-fourth teaspoon nutmeg or any extract and bake one and one-quarter hours. If you can spare it, beat one egg and add to the pudding fifteen minutes before serving.

MRS. MARTHA STRUDWICK, BELMAR, N. J.

Indian Tapioca

Mix together one-third cup tapioca and one-fourth cup Indian meal and stir while sprinkling into one quart scalded milk. Stir and cook until the tapioca becomes transparent, then stir into the pudding one cup molasses, one-half teaspoon salt, two tablespoons butter and turn into a buttered baking dish. Pour over the top one and one-half cups cold milk and set in the oven without stirring. Bake about an hour. Serve with or without cream.

MRS. J. L. LINDBERG, WORCESTER, MASS.

Apple Tapioca

One cup Larkin Pearl Tapioca, one-half teaspoon salt, one-half cup sugar, one-half teaspoon nutmeg and five apples. Wash the tapioca in cold water, soak over night in six cups water. Put in Larkin Double-Boiler, add the salt and sugar. Cook one hour. Put a layer of tapioca in a baking dish, then a layer of apples pared and sliced. Sprinkle with nutmeg and sugar. Cover with tapioca and bake until apples are tender (about forty-five minutes). Serve with whipped or plain cream. This dish is very pretty if the tapioca is colored a light red with Larkin Culinary Paste.

MRS. EMERY CHRISTENSEN, MOROCCO, IND.

Pineapple Tapioca

Take one cup Larkin Pearl Tapioca, cover with water, soak over night. In the morning add one-half cup water, cook until clear. Add one pint diced pineapple, juice of two lemons and one cup sugar. Take from the fire, fold in whites of three eggs beaten quite stiff. Serve with whipped cream or sweet sauce. This is fine.

MRS. A. L. MILLER, ELEROY, ILL.

Tapioca Cream

Put one-fourth cup Larkin. Pearl Tapioca into double-boiler. Cover with cold water and soak one hour. Drain off water, add two cups milk and cook until tapioca is soft and transparent. Add the yolks of two eggs beaten with one-third cup Larkin Sugar. Add one-fourth teaspoon salt. Add part of the tapioca mixture to the eggs. Put back into sauce-pan. Cook for three minutes or until it thickens. Remove from fire, add the stiffly-beaten whites of two eggs, flavor with one-half teaspoon each of lemon and orange extract. Serve with or without cream.

MRS. WALTER F. BARRINGER, NEWARK, N. J.

Brown Betty

In a quart pudding-dish arrange alternate layers of sliced apples and bread-crumbs; season each layer with bits of butter, a little sugar and a pinch each of ground cinnamon, cloves and allspice. When the dish is full pour over it one-half cup each of molasses and water mixed; cover the top with crumbs. Place the dish in a pan containing hot water and bake three-fourths of an hour. Serve with any sweet sauce.

MRS. JENNIE L. THOMAS, AMSTERDAM, N. Y.

Coffee Corn Starch

Four tablespoons each of sugar and corn starch, one cup of left-over Larkin Coffee, one cup milk, one-fourth teaspoon salt. Mix corn starch and sugar with a little of the cold milk. Scald remainder of milk with the coffee. Pour slowly on corn starch mixture. Cook in double-boiler stirring until it thickens. Cover and cook ten minutes. Pour into wet mold and chill. Serve with whipped cream.

M. L. LINDSAY, ALLSTON, MASS.

Strawberry Shortcake

Make a biscuit crust with two cups Larkin Flour sifted twice with two teaspoons baking powder and one-half teaspoon salt; rub in two tablespoons each of butter and lard. Mix with one-half cup milk, use a little flour to keep it from sticking to the hands and put into a pie-tin. Bake in a quick oven. When done, split apart and butter each half. Then spread with strawberries prepared as follows: To one quart berries allow one cup sugar; mash sugar and berries. Let stand an hour or two. Before using, beat the white of one egg and stir into the berries. Spread between the cake, put a generous supply on top and cover the whole with whipped cream.

MRS. MARY E. DAVIDSON, MELROSE, MASS.

Raspberry Blanc Mange

Heat one and one-half cups milk in a double-boiler; add one-half cup sugar. Mix six tablespoons Larkin Corn Starch with one-half cup milk, add to the scalded milk, stir until it thickens. Cook ten minutes, add one-half teaspoon Larkin Vanilla Flavoring Extract and one-fourth teaspoon Larkin Salt (the blanc mange may be colored a light pink with Larkin Cherry-Red Culinary Paste). Put a layer of Larkin Raspberry Jam into the bottom of a glass dish. When cold turn the blanc mange onto it, sprinkle with Larkin Shredded Cocoanut and it is ready to serve.

MISS VERA LAVERTY, LOMERVILLE, MASS.

Rye and Raspberries

Dilute one cup rye flour with one cup water or milk. Add two cups scalded milk, one teaspoon salt and three-fourths cup sugar. Cook in double-boiler one hour or in fireless cooker several hours. Serve with ripe raspberries and milk or cream. A delicious and wholesome dessert or breakfast dish.

MISS ALICE GRADY, NEW HAVEN, CONN.

Bavarian Cream

Prepare one package Larkin Orange Jelly Dessert using the juice from one can of Larkin Pineapple and water sufficient to make one and one-half cups; add one-half cup sugar, the juice of one lemon and enough Larkin Cherry-Red Culinary Paste to give a pretty pink color. Put aside to cool. When it begins to thicken, add one cup of cream whipped until stiff. Pour into a pan rinsed with cold water; have the jelly one inch thick. When firm cut in small squares, lay on each square a slice of pineapple, cover the pineapple with whipped sweetened cream. Decorate with cherries and sprinkle with chopped nuts

MRS. J. M. MARTIN, COLUMBIA, TENN.

Orange Dessert

Arrange layers of sliced oranges, sprinkle each layer with Larkin Powdered Sugar and Shredded Cocoanut. Sliced oranges when served alone should not stand long after slicing, as they are apt to become bitter. This may be served as a salad or dessert.

MRS. G. W. FOGG, CRESTON, IOWA.

Marshmallow Dessert

Cut one-half pound each of Larkin Marshmallows and walnuts in small pieces. Whip one-half pint cream, sweeten and flavor to taste. Serve in sherbet glasses with a tiny piece of jelly or a Maraschino cherry on top.

MRS. ALONZO BAILEY, ISLAND POND, VT.

Maple Cream Sponge

Soak one-fourth box of Larkin Gelatine in cold water until soft. Dissolve in one cup hot milk, add one-third cup sugar and one-half teaspoon vanilla. When gelatine is beginning to thicken, stir it up and fold in lightly one pint whipped cream to which has been added one cup maple syrup and one-half cup chopped walnut meats. Put on ice and serve when firm.

L. G. Partridge, Spofford, N. H.

Rice Jelly Sponge

Boil one-fourth cup Larkin Rice. Drain off the water, add one pint milk, one-half cup sugar; when quite hot, add two tablespoons gelatine softened in one-half cup water. Stir over the fire two minutes. Set aside to cool. When cool fold in one-half pint whipped cream flavored with one teaspoon Larkin Vanilla. Pour into a mold. Serve with canned strawberries, raspberries or peaches.

Mrs. Oran C. Balcom, Natick, Mass.

Prune Jelly

Soak one pound of prunes over night, the next day cook until tender. Remove the stones and add a little sugar. Make a plain jelly with one-half package Larkin Gelatine; when beginning to set add the prunes and the stiffly beaten white of one egg. Serve with cream or custard sauce.

Mrs. R. E. Chace, Somerset, Mass.

Baked Apples with Sauce

Wash and core six large apples. Fill the centers with sugar and cinnamon. Pour a little water over the apples. Bake in moderate oven. Make a sauce with one and one-half cups of milk, one-half cup sugar, one and one-half tablespoons Larkin Corn Starch and one egg. Flavor with vanilla. Serve warm for supper.

Mrs. A. Wiltmann, Pearl River, N. Y.

Dainty Dessert

Prepare one box of Larkin Gelatine according to directions, put away to chill. When just setting beat up gelatine with a fork or egg-beater and add one and one-half pounds of Larkin Marshmallows cut in small pieces, one dozen macaroons crumbled with the hands, or clipped with scissors in small pieces, one-quarter pound of almonds coarsely chopped. When well mixed fold in one and one-half pints of cream whipped quite stiff and flavored with any extract. When quite firm it is ready to serve. These quantities will serve twenty people.

Mrs. C. E. Chamberlain, East Providence, R. I.

FROZEN DESSERTS

Frozen desserts are easily and quickly made and are both cooling and refreshing. To make the work as easy as possible a good freezer, a burlap bag, a wooden mallet or an axe, a dipper or sauce-pan, ice and coarse rock salt are needed.

Put the ice into the bag and crush fine—the freezing will be accomplished in much less time if the ice is quite fine. Place can containing the mixture in freezer and turn the crank to be sure it fits properly, then pack around it solidly with salt and ice, using three level measures of ice to one of salt. If only a small amount is to be frozen, the ice and salt need not come to the top of the can. In winter snow may be used in place of ice. Never have the can more than three-fourths full as the mixture increases in bulk during freezing, and if the can is overcrowded, the cream will be coarse-grained. Turn the crank slowly and steadily to expose as large surface of mixture as possible to ice and salt. Never draw off the salt water until mixture is frozen, unless it is apt to get into the can, because the salt water hastens the freezing. After mixture is frozen, draw off the water, remove the dasher, and with a spoon pack solidly or place in a mold as preferred, put cork in opening in cover and repack, using four level measures of ice to one of salt. Place an old piece of carpet over the top. When ready to serve, run cool water over the can to wash off salty water.

ICE-CREAMS AND SHERBETS

Ice-Cream with Milk

Three eggs, three quarts milk, two cups sugar, one-fourth package gelatine, two teaspoons extract. Soak the gelatine five minutes in one cup milk, scald the balance of one quart; add the eggs to this; cook until thick; now add the softened gelatine. Add the milk and any extract preferred. Crushed fruit or fruit juice may be used with this if liked. These quantities make one gallon of cream. MRS. J. K. FOSTER, SEAFORD, VA.

New Idea Ice-Cream

Moisten the contents of one package Larkin Prepared Pudding in three-fourths cup cold milk. Scald the remainder of a quart of milk; into it stir the moistened powder. Cook ten minutes. Remove from fire, stir in two eggs beaten light and one quart milk. Add one-fourth teaspoon salt and one tablespoon of any extract. If you can spare it, add one cup cream. Freeze. This will serve twelve people. MRS. GRACE GAY, BROCKTON, MASS.

Coffee Ice-Cream

Scald two quarts milk. Beat the yolks of six eggs and two cups sugar together until light. Add them to the scalded milk. Stir and cook for ten minutes, take from the fire and add one pint cream. Stir constantly for two minutes, then add one-half cup Larkin Ground Coffee and stand on the stove until thoroughly heated. Stand aside until cool. Strain and freeze.

MRS. FRANK S. MERRILL, BRISTOL, CONN.

Orange Ice-Cream

Use two pint-size cans of Larkin Evaporated Milk; add an equal amount of water that has previously been boiled and cooled and one pound sugar. Flavor with three teaspoons Larkin Orange Flavoring Extract. Mix together well and freeze in a Larkin Ice-Cream Freezer. This makes about two quarts of delicious ice-cream. Any other flavoring desired may be used.

MRS. E. G. KORAHEK, CHICAGO, ILL.

Fruit Cream with Gelatine

Soften one-quarter box Larkin Gelatine in one cup milk. Scald the remainder of one quart milk. Add one and one-half cups sugar to milk and pour over the gelatine. Flavor with one and one-half teaspoons of any Larkin Flavoring Extract. Add a pinch of salt. When cold add one pint cream (whipped). Freeze in Larkin Ice-Cream Freezer. When frozen remove the dasher, repack and allow to ripen about two hours, that the ingredients may be well blended. One pint of any kind of crushed fruit may be used with this.

MRS. ROY S. HEATWOLE, HARRISONBURG, VA.

Lemon Sherbet

Juice of four lemons, grated rind of two, one quart water, three cups Larkin Sugar, one-fourth package Larkin Gelatine, one teaspoon Larkin Vanilla Flavoring Extract, white of one egg. To the lemon juice and rind, add the sugar. Soak the gelatine in one-half cup cold water. Dissolve by standing in a pan of hot water. Thoroughly mix all ingredients and when partly frozen add the stiffly-beaten white of egg. Freeze again. Fruit may be added to this if desired.

MRS. I. F. HURT, ROANOKE, VA.

Milk Sherbet

Two quarts milk, juice of six oranges and one large lemon, sugar to sweeten, one-fourth teaspoon salt. Mix juice and sugar. Stir constantly while adding milk; freeze and serve.

JOSEPHINE MURPHY, ROXBURY, MASS.

Peach Sherbet

One quart canned peaches, one quart cream, one and one-half pints water, two cups sugar, whites of three eggs. Put the peaches through a sieve or colander, add sugar and water, then the cream. When partly frozen add the beaten whites of the eggs. This quantity makes one gallon in a Larkin Freezer and is delicious.

MRS. MARY SLEE, MUNCY, PA.

Chocolate Mousse

Put one ounce or square of unsweetened chocolate into a small sauce-pan with one-fourth cup sugar; add one tablespoon boiling water, and stir over the fire until smooth. Add a few spoons of cream to this mixture and whip the remainder of a pint of cream until quite stiff. Sweeten the cream with three-fourths cup sugar; add one tablespoon vanilla extract and the chocolate mixture to the cream. Pour into chilled mold and pack in a wooden pail for three hours using equal parts of ice and salt.

DAISY E. LIGHT, MARTINSBURG, WEST VA.

Fruit Mousse

Whip one pint cream; add one pint Larkin Canned Fruit or preserves and mix well with cream; pack in ice or snow and leave three or four hours.

MRS. R. E. SMITH, MILAN, PA.

Maple Syrup Cream

Dilute six tablespoons corn starch in cold milk, scald the balance of three pints in double-boiler; add corn starch; cook ten minutes. Add yolks of three eggs; cook three minutes, then add stiffly-beaten whites. Remove from the fire; add two cups Larkin Maple Syrup. When quite cold add one pint cream; one tablespoon vanilla extract and one cup hickory or walnut meats finely chopped or put through food-chopper. The nuts are not necessary but improve the flavor. Freeze when quite cold.

MRS. RAY F. COSSENTINE, SUSQUEHANNA, PA.

Pie-Crust

Two cups sifted flour, one-half cup lard, one-fourth cup ice-water, one-half teaspoon salt. Cut the lard into the flour with a knife until thoroughly mixed, then stir in the water. Do not touch with the hands until this is done. Turn it on a board and roll quite thin using as little flour as possible in the rolling; fold and roll out again, and continue the folding and rolling for two or three minutes. Everything should be very cold and the hands used as little as possible.

Elizabeth G. Leary, West Chester, Pa.

Baking Powder Crust

Sift together two and one-half cups Larkin Flour, one and one-half teaspoons baking powder, one-half teaspoon Larkin Salt, one-half cup Larkin Corn Starch. Chop in three-fourths cup Larkin Lard with a Larkin Spatula. When thoroughly mixed, add enough cold water to mix to a firm dough. Roll out quickly and lightly. Enough for two pies.

Mrs. Barnett M. Rhetta, Baltimore, Md.

Raisin Turnovers

Two cups Larkin Pastry Flour, three-fourths cup Larkin Pure Lard, one-half teaspoon salt, ice-water to mix. Sift flour and salt together in a wooden bowl; chop shortening in thoroughly; add ice-water to mix. Roll out, fold evenly into three layers; turn half around and roll again. Repeat twice. This makes it flaky. Cut out with a saucer. Place one tablespoon of raisin filling on one-half; prick and turn over the upper half and pinch edges together.

To Make the Raisin Filling:

Juice and grated rind of one lemon, one cup Larkin Seeded Raisins, three Larkin Soda Crackers, one cup Larkin Granulated Sugar, one egg, two tablespoons cold water. Chop raisins and crackers, beat egg and sugar, then mix all together. One-half cup chopped walnuts or pecans added to the filling is a great improvement. These are excellent for a picnic, as they carry nicely.

Grace E. Miller, Eustis, Fla.

Peanut Butter Pin-Wheels

Two cups flour sifted with one-half teaspoon salt and two teaspoons Larkin Baking Powder. Work into this one-half cup lard and mix to a dough with milk. Roll out lightly into a long wide strip. Mix one-fourth cup peanut butter with two tablespoons water, add a few grains of salt, spread with a spatula. Roll up as for jelly roll. Cut in slices one-fourth inch thick. Bake in a hot oven.

MRS. HENRY R. SPENCER, GRANVILLE, N. Y.

Crust Cake

Mix together two cups Larkin Powdered Sugar, two cups Larkin Flour, two teaspoons Larkin Baking Powder, two eggs beaten, one-half cup butter and one-half cup milk; add one-half teaspoon Larkin Vanilla. Put in pie-plates lined with pie-crust. Sprinkle the cakes well with powdered sugar before putting in oven to bake. This will make four ordinary-sized cakes. When done they will look like a pie.

MRS. GEORGE OWENS, PHILADELPHIA, PA.

Cheese Straws

Two and one-half cups pastry flour, one and one-half teaspoons salt, one-half teaspoon baking powder, three-fourths cup water, one-half pound cheese (put through food-chopper) one teaspoon paprika, two-thirds cup shortening. Mix and roll as for pastry. Cut in strips five inches long and one-fourth inch wide. Bake eight minutes in hot oven. Pile log-cabin fashion and serve with salad or coffee. These quantities make ninety cheese straws.

MRS. DAVID DAVIES, REMSEN, N. Y.

Lemon Cheese

One-fourth pound butter, six eggs well beaten, juice and grated rind of three lemons. Mix and put over a slow fire, stir all the time. When thick as honey add two cups sugar and cook a little longer. Pour into jars, seal and it will keep for six months. If it is not required to keep, use less sugar. This makes a nice filling for tarts or jelly cakes.

MRS. F. RICHARDSON, SANTA ROSA, FLA.

Lemon Sponge Pie

One cup sugar, three tablespoons butter, yolks of two eggs. Beat these together. Add juice and grated rind of one lemon, three tablespoons flour, mix all together, add one cup milk and the stiffly-beaten whites of the eggs. Bake three-fourths of an hour in slow oven using only one crust.

MRS. R. V. BUCKAGE, VINCENTOWN, N. J.

Lemon Pie

One lemon, one cup sugar, three tablespoons corn starch, two eggs, one pint hot water, one tablespoon butter. Dilute corn starch in cold water, put sugar, butter and grated rind and juice of lemon into a sauce-pan, add corn starch and cook for ten minutes; then add the yolks of eggs slightly beaten, cook until thickened, cool, pour into pie-shell, beat whites of eggs very stiff, add two tablespoons sugar, spread on top of pie and brown slightly in cool oven.

MRS. HARRY W. TYLER, TOANO, VA.

Lemon and Other Tarts

Line patty-pans with ordinary pastry and put one teaspoon of the following mixture into each pan. Mix together thoroughly one egg, one cup sugar, one teaspoon melted butter, juice of one lemon. Bake in hot oven. A good filling for cooked tart-shells is Larkin Prepared Pudding with a spoonful of whipped cream on top. Larkin Prepared Jelly Dessert also makes a dainty dessert served in the same way. When strawberries are in season crush a few berries, sweeten to taste and serve in baked shells with whipped cream. These desserts are suitable to use after a heavy meal and also inexpensive.

MRS. ANNIE E. CAMPBELL, (NO ADDRESS GIVEN)

Lemon Crumb Pie

One cup sugar, one cup cold water, one cup fine bread-crumbs (or one thick slice of bread), juice and rind of one lemon, two eggs, pinch of salt, two tablespoons butter. Cover the bread with the water, leave for twenty minutes, add the egg yolks slightly beaten, juice and rind of lemon, butter, salt and sugar. Mix thoroughly, line a pie-plate with good pastry, pour in the filling, bake thirty minutes in hot oven, cover with meringue made with whites of two eggs and two tablespoons sugar. I have used this recipe for thirty-eight years.

MRS. P. C. BROPHY, MOUNTAIN GROVE, MO.

Eggless Rhubarb-Lemon Pie

Stir together one cup stewed rhubarb, two cups boiling water, one and one-half cups Larkin Sugar, add eight tablespoons Larkin Corn Starch blended with one-half cup cold water. Cook over boiling water ten minutes, stir frequently. Add three tablespoons butter, one teaspoon Larkin Lemon Flavoring Extract. Pour into two ready-baked crusts. Serve when cold. These are delicious.

MISS J. MAUD GRAYBILL, BUCHANAN, VA.

Plain Custard Pie

Whether for a pie or to bake plain in a dish, allow three eggs to every pint of milk with one-third cup of sugar; beat sufficiently to mix; flavor with one-half teaspoon vanilla or a little nutmeg. Bake in slow oven. One-half cup Larkin Shredded Cocoanut may be sprinkled over custard if liked.

MRS. WM. HESS, ST. LOUIS, MO.

Cream, Banana or Cocoanut Pie

Cover two deep pie-pans with a rich crust, pinch here and there and bake in a hot oven. Mix together one-third cup flour with three-fourths cup sugar and a pinch of salt. Add one pint scalded milk and three tablespoons butter. Cook five minutes, add the beaten yolks of two eggs gradually to thickened milk. Cook a few minutes stirring constantly. Set aside to cool, add one teaspoon orange extract and fill prepared crusts. Make a meringue of the whites of the eggs whipped very stiff, and one-fourth cup of sugar, spread on pies and set in oven to brown. Delicious. For banana pie add three sliced bananas to the mixture. For cocoanut add one-half cup Larkin Shredded Cocoanut.

MRS. HOWARD DOUGLAS, WAMPUM, PA.

Eggless Cream Pie

Mix together three-fourths cup sugar and four tablespoons Larkin Corn Starch. Add two cups scalded milk, one tablespoon butter. Cook in double-boiler ten minutes, take from fire, add one teaspoon Larkin Lemon Flavoring Extract. Pour into baked pie-crust and sprinkle top with Larkin Shredded Cocoanut.

MRS. THOMAS H. RUNYON, RICHMOND, IND.

Sour Cream Raisin Pie

Line a pie-tin with rich pie-crust and fill with the following mixture: One cup Larkin Raisins chopped, one cup Larkin Sugar, yolks of three eggs, one cup sour cream, pinch of salt, one teaspoon Larkin Cinnamon. Bake slowly, use the three whites for meringue. This makes an excellent pie.

MRS. W. R. STEUERWALD, ESTELLINE, S. DAK.

Raisin and Rhubarb Pie

One cup raisins, one and one-half cups rhubarb cut very small, one cup sugar, one-half teaspoon Larkin Salt, one tablespoon flour, (rolled cracker may be used instead of flour if preferred), one egg. Mix thoroughly and bake in two crusts.

MRS. FLORENCE G. CHIPMAN, ATTLEBORO, MASS.

Red Currant Pie

Mix together yolks of two eggs, two tablespoons flour, one cup sugar, add one cup ripe red currants mashed. Bake in a single crimped-edge crust in a shallow pie-pan. When baked cover with a meringue made with whites of two eggs stiffly-beaten, and two tablespoons granulated sugar. Brown in slow oven.

Mrs. J. Warren Merrell, Three Rivers, Mass.

Date Pie

Cook three-fourths cup dates with two cups milk for twenty minutes. Strain, rub through a sieve. Add two beaten eggs and one-fourth teaspoon salt and a few grains of nutmeg. Line pie-plate with pastry and bake with one crust in the lower part of a fairly hot oven.

Mrs. Robert Paterson, South Paris, Maine.

Fig Pie

Put one cup molasses, one cup sugar, the grated rind of one lemon, one-half pound Larkin Figs cut fine or put through food-chopper, and two cups water, into double-boiler; cook for twenty minutes. Thicken with four tablespoons flour, add one beaten egg. Have pie-shells baked ready. This is sufficient for two pies.

Mrs. Pearl Main, Ingersoll, Okla.

Prune Pie

Cook one-half pound prunes without sugar, remove stones, cut prunes in quarters, and mix with one-half cup sugar. Add one tablespoon lemon juice. Cook down the prune juice until you have about three tablespoons. Spread pie-pan with pastry, cover with prunes, pour over the juice, dot with butter, dredge with flour, put on upper crust and bake in hot oven.

Larkin Kitchen.

Prune Cream Pie

Stew gently one-half pound Larkin Prunes which have been soaked over night. Stone and mash prunes through a colander. Add to the cup of pulp one cup thin cream (or milk). Mix one teaspoon Larkin Corn Starch with one-third cup of Larkin Granulated Sugar, add the yolks of two well-beaten eggs and one teaspoon of Larkin Vanilla. Line a pie-plate with pie-crust, fill with mixture and bake quickly. Beat the whites of the eggs stiff, add two tablespoons granulated sugar, spread over the pie, return the pie to the oven and brown lightly. This is delicious.

Mrs. Edw. R. Sechrist, Blossburg, Pa.

Mock Cherry Pie

One-half cup raisins, one cup cranberries, one-half cup hot water, one cup sugar, one tablespoon flour, one teaspoon Larkin Vanilla. Pour the hot water over the raisins and cranberries and cook till the cranberries burst, then add the sugar and flour. Take from the fire, add the vanilla. Bake with two crusts. This makes one pie. If you wish, the cranberries may be cut open and washed in cold water to remove seeds.

MRS. L. O. COGAN, RAVENNA, OHIO.

Pineapple Pie

Put one cup Larkin Pineapple cut in dice, one cup water or pineapple juice and one-half cup sugar into a sauce-pan. Bring to a boil, then add two tablespoons corn starch mixed with a little cold water, boil until thick and clear. Pour into previously-baked crust. When cool cover with whipped cream or a one-egg meringue. This makes two small pies.

MRS. FRED COLE, CUBA, N. Y.

Carrot Pie

Add one cup grated raw carrots, to one cup sweet milk, one tablespoon melted butter, one teaspoon Larkin Cinnamon, one-half teaspoon Larkin Ginger, beat together the yolks of two eggs and one-half cup sugar. Bake with one crust. Use whites of two eggs and little sugar for frosting.

MISS ANNA FAUCETT, SONORA, N. Y.

Rice Pie, Belgium Style

Cook one-half cup Larkin Rice with milk in double-boiler until tender, add sugar to taste, take from fire and cool. Now beat six eggs until light, flavor with Larkin Vanilla or Lemon, add eggs to rice and mix all together. It will be like a thin custard. Make a good pie-crust using Larkin Flour and Lard. Fill with the rice custard, bake in moderate oven until custard is set. This will make three large pies without top crust.

MRS. P. F. MCGONIGAL, WEST PHILADELPHIA, PA.

Cocoanut Pie without Crust

Beat two eggs, add two tablespoons sugar and four tablespoons flour smoothed with a little milk. Add the balance of pint of milk, one cup Larkin Shredded Cocoanut, one-fourth teaspoon salt, one-half teaspoon vanilla. Put into a pie-pan and bake in moderate oven. Insert a knife on the side and when it is done it will have formed a crust. This is quickly made and is very good.

MISS J. M. STEPHENS, JERSEY CITY, N. J.

Cocoanut Custard Pie

One pint milk, one cup Larkin Shredded Cocoanut, one-half cup sugar, yolks of three eggs. Beat yolks with sugar and then stir in milk and cocoanut, fill crust even full, bake in medium oven. Beat whites of eggs to a stiff froth and add three tablespoons powdered sugar, spread over pie and bake a light brown. Excellent.

MRS. JOS. I. SMITH, LEIPSIC, OHIO.

Butter Scotch Pie

One cup Larkin Brown Sugar, two eggs, two tablespoons flour, one cup cold water, two tablespoons butter, one teaspoon Larkin Vanilla. Mix sugar and flour together, add the water gradually and stir over the fire until thick. Add the egg yolks and butter, then vanilla. Fill baked crust, beat the whites of eggs to a stiff froth, add two tablespoons sugar. Put this on top and brown in slow oven.

MRS. EDGAR GOTSCHALL, JACKSONVILLE, ILL.

Two-Egg Chocolate Pie

Melt one ounce Larkin Unsweetened Chocolate in one cup boiling water; add one cup granulated sugar and two tablespoons Larkin Corn Starch mixed together. Cook ten minutes, add beaten yolks of two eggs and two tablespoons butter. Flavor with one teaspoon Larkin Vanilla. Make a meringue with whites of eggs and sugar, brown daintily. When eggs are scarce use double quantity of corn starch and leave out eggs.

FLORENCE A. RICHARDSON, TOPEKA, KANS.

Chess Pie

Heat one cup milk in a double-boiler, add one-third cup sugar and two teaspoons butter. Mix two tablespoons corn starch, one-half teaspoon each of cinnamon and allspice with a little cold milk. Cook three minutes, then add yolks of two eggs, cook two minutes longer and pour into a baked pie-shell. Beat the egg whites, add sugar and brown in oven.

MRS. E. J. BURKE, NECK, MO.

Buttermilk Pie

Mix five tablespoons flour with one-half cup buttermilk until smooth. Beat two eggs until mixed, add three-fourths cup sugar and four tablespoons butter, add one and one-half cups buttermilk, one teaspoon lemon extract. Mix thoroughly. Line a large pie-pan with pastry and pour in the custard, bake in moderate oven. Larkin Shredded Cocoanut sprinkled over the pie gives a pretty finish.

EMMA M. SUTTLE, GALETON, PA.

Vinegar Pie

One egg, three tablespoons Larkin Cider Vinegar, one teaspoon Larkin Lemon Flavoring Extract, four tablespoons flour, one cup sugar, one cup water. Mix sugar and flour thoroughly together, then add boiling water, cook five minutes, add egg well beaten, cook in double-boiler two minutes, add lemon and vinegar, put into pie-crust which should be already baked. If preferred the yolk only may be used in the pie and the white for meringue.

MRS. CLIFF HARRIS, MAXWELL, ILL.

Mince-Meat

Two pounds beef from the shoulder, one pound suet, five pounds apples, one pound mixed candied peel, three pounds raisins, two pounds currants, two and one-half pounds brown sugar, two tablespoons Larkin Cinnamon, one tablespoon each of cloves, allspice, salt and nutmeg, one quart cider and one pint molasses. Cook the beef until tender. When cool put through the food-chopper. Also the suet. Peel the apples and chop, not too fine (be sure you have five pounds after they are chopped) steam the candied peel awhile over hot water, then shave off in strips. Pick over the raisins, wash the currants, add the sugar and mix all the ingredients together (I always use cider that has been boiled down). If it is too stiff you can add more molasses. Do not cook but put into glass jars and seal up and it is ready for use. This is fine and will keep all through the winter months.

MARIE GEHRKE, HERINGTON, KANS.

Old-Fashioned Mince-Meat

Four pounds beef (boiled), three pounds suet (kidney preferred), eight pounds chopped apples, three pounds Larkin Currants washed and dried, three pounds Larkin Seeded Raisins washed and dried, six pounds Larkin Yellow Sugar, two pounds citron cut fine, one cup Larkin Strawberry Jam, one cup Larkin Raspberry Jam, the grated rind and juice of two oranges and four lemons, four tablespoons Larkin Cinnamon, one tablespoon each Larkin Cloves, mace and Allspice, two Larkin Nutmegs grated, two quarts Larkin Grape Juice, one pint Larkin Molasses. Cook meat in the least possible amount of water, chop very fine. Remove all membrane from suet, dredge with Larkin Flour, chop and mix with meat. Season with Larkin Salt, add to this all other ingredients; cider may be added if desired. This must not be cooked. This makes a very large quantity.

MRS. D. H. DAGER, LAFAYETTE HILL, PA.

Tomato Mince-Meat

Chop one peck green tomatoes or put them through food-chopper using coarse cutter, drain off juice and add as much water as there was juice; also add five pounds brown sugar and two pounds chopped Larkin Raisins. Cook slowly until the tomatoes are tender, then add two tablespoons each of Larkin Cloves, Cinnamon, Allspice and Salt; also one cup Larkin Vinegar. Boil until thick, stirring frequently, then add six large sour apples that have been peeled, cored and chopped. When the apples are done the mince-meat is ready for the jars. Seal while hot. You will find this very delicious for pies.

Mrs. J. A. Henry, Strawberry Point, Iowa.

Mock Mince Pie

Mix together one and one-half cups Larkin Granulated Sugar, one cup Larkin Seeded Raisins chopped, two cups bread-crumbs, two cups water, one-half cup Larkin Cider Vinegar and one teaspoon each of Larkin Cinnamon, Cloves and All-spice. Place on stove and cook until thick. One beaten egg may be added if you can spare it. Bake in two crusts.

Mrs. J. A. Henry, Strawberry Point, Iowa.

Pumpkin Pie

Take two cups Larkin Canned Pumpkin, two cups milk, one-half cup sugar, one-half teaspoon ginger and nutmeg, one teaspoon cinnamon, one-half teaspoon salt and two eggs. Beat eggs with sugar and spices, mix all together; bake in moderate oven about forty-five minutes. Squash pie is made in exactly the same way.

Mrs. Viana J. Luchringer, Great Barrington, Mass.

Tomato Sauce

Put one cup Larkin Canned Tomatoes into a sauce-pan with one cup water, two whole cloves, four peppercorns, two sprigs parsley, one tablespoon chopped onion. Simmer for thirty minutes, strain and thicken with three tablespoons butter and three tablespoons flour blended together. Add hot stock gradually. Cook a few minutes, add pepper and salt to taste.

MRS. H. F. RIEMER, DETROIT, MICH.

Cranberry Sauce

One pint water, one pint sugar. Boil five minutes, then add one quart cranberries and boil fifteen minutes. Place on back of stove for one hour. They are then ready to serve.

MRS. KIMBALL P. RYAN, CHATHAM PORT, MASS.

Peanut Butter Sauce

Melt one tablespoon butter and two of Larkin Peanut Butter in a small sauce-pan. When softened, add three tablespoons flour and two cups milk. Stir until boiling, cook five minutes, add half a teaspoon Larkin Salt and a little pepper. This is sufficient to serve with two cups boiled macaroni or noodles. Delicious with plain, boiled or steamed rice.

MRS. T. F. SARGENT, SPRINGFIELD, ILL.

Cream Sauce

Two tablespoons butter, two tablespoons flour, one-half teaspoon salt, a few grains of pepper, one cup milk. Melt the butter, stir in the flour and cook until bubbling, add the milk, stir constantly over the fire until it reaches the boiling point; add the salt and pepper and it is ready for use.

LARKIN KITCHEN.

Apple Sauce

One pound apples (or four medium size), one-half pint water, one-half cup sugar. Quarter and core the apples, do not pare them, add the water, cover sauce-pan and bring to the boiling point. Press through a colander, add the sugar, then turn out to cool. Serve with duck, goose or roasted pork.

LARKIN KITCHEN.

Egg Sauce

This is made by adding two hard-boiled eggs, chopped fine, to one pint cream sauce.

LARKIN KITCHEN.

Drawn Butter Sauce

Make in exactly the same way as cream sauce using water in place of milk. With the addition of one tablespoon vinegar, this makes a good fish sauce.

LARKIN KITCHEN.

Caper Sauce

Make in the same way as drawn butter, adding one tablespoon of capers. Serve with boiled mutton.

LARKIN KITCHEN.

Vanilla Sauce

Mix one-half cup sugar and one tablespoon corn starch; add gradually one cup boiling water, stirring constantly; boil ten minutes, remove from fire; add two tablespoons butter and one teaspoon vanilla or any other extract.

MRS. C. CRANE, DES MOINES, IOWA.

Lemon Sauce

Blend two tablespoons corn starch with one cup sugar, add gradually one and one-half cups hot water, stirring constantly. Cook ten minutes then add one-fourth cup butter, the beaten yolks of two eggs and the grated rind and juice of one lemon.

BESSIE OSBORN, BORING, MD.

Eggless Lemon Sauce

One-half cup sugar, one cup boiling water, one tablespoon corn starch or one and one-half tablespoons flour, two tablespoons butter, one and one-half tablespoons lemon juice, few gratings of nutmeg. Mix sugar and corn starch, add water gradually, stirring constantly; boil ten minutes, remove from fire, add butter, lemon juice and nutmeg. If you have no fresh lemons, use Larkin Lemon Flavoring Extract.

MRS. HANNAH LLOYD, ALLOWAY, N. J.

Orange Sauce

Mix together two cups sugar, one egg, two tablespoons cream, one tablespoon soft butter and one-half teaspoon orange extract. Serve with any plain pudding.

MISS ELSIE A. BINGHAM, BROOKLYN, N. Y.

Custard Sauce

Beat three eggs slightly, add one-fourth cup sugar and a pinch of salt; stir while adding gradually two cups hot milk. Cook in double-boiler, continue stirring until mixture thickens and a coating is formed on the spoon. Strain immediately; chill and add one-half teaspoon Larkin Vanilla or Almond Flavoring Extract. When eggs are scarce, use yolk of one egg and two tablespoons corn starch.

EDITH RYDER, RICHMONDVILLE, N. Y.

Foamy Sauce

Beat whites of two eggs, until light. Add one-half cup sugar and beat until stiff. Whip one-half cup thick sweet cream, add to sauce with one teaspoon, vanilla or any extract. Delicious.

MRS. PHILIP C. STORY, THREE RIVERS, MASS.

Mock Cream Sauce

Two tablespoons Larkin Corn Starch, two tablespoons sugar, two cups milk, one teaspoon Larkin Vanilla, whites of two eggs. Mix corn starch and sugar, add hot milk, cook ten minutes, cool. Add vanilla and stiffly-beaten whites of eggs. Serve with any pudding that requires cream.

ALICIA NOVA, BUFFALO, N. Y.

Chocolate Sauce

Two ounces chocolate, two cups milk, one-half cup sugar, two tablespoons corn starch, one teaspoon vanilla. Put milk into a double-boiler with the chocolate, stir until smooth and melted, moisten the corn starch with a little cold milk; add hot milk, cook until smooth and thick; add the sugar; take from the fire and add vanilla. Serve with cottage pudding or blanc mange.

C. M. SMALL, SOUTH HARWICH, MASS.

Hard Sauce

One-half cup butter, one cup powdered sugar, one-half teaspoon lemon and vanilla extract mixed, or a little nutmeg. Cream butter, add sugar and extract gradually. Form into a roll and slice or serve by the spoonful.

LARKIN KITCHEN.

Fruit Sauce

To one-pint can of fruit allow one cup whipping cream. Drain the fruit and rub through a sieve, whip the cream and fold into the pulp; sweeten if necessary. Apricots, strawberries or raspberries may be used. Delicious with plain layer cake or hot biscuits.

LARKIN KITCHEN.

Tomato Catsup

Wash ripe tomatoes. Cut in four pieces and boil until soft. Remove from fire and when cool enough to handle strain through a coarse sieve. Measure, and to every five quarts of juice allow one and one-half pints Larkin Vinegar, one tablespoon each Larkin Black Pepper and Cinnamon and two and one-half tablespoons Larkin Salt. Mix one-half tablespoon Larkin Mustard in two tablespoons cold water; add to other ingredients. Put on fire to boil. After boiling one-half hour add one and two-thirds cups Larkin Granulated Sugar. Boil down to about three-fourths the original quantity. Remove and bottle at once. Seal air-tight with Larkin Paraffin Wax.

MRS. FLORENCE HALL, NATICK, MASS.

Cooked French Mustard

Three tablespoons each Larkin Mustard and Sugar. Beat one egg light, mix smooth with one cup diluted vinegar, cook a few minutes, add one tablespoon butter as you remove from stove.

MRS. CHARLES W. COOLEY, EAST WHATELY, MASS.

Watermelon Rind Pickle

Pare off very carefully the green part of the rind of a good ripe watermelon, trim off all the red part, cut in pieces two inches in length, place in a porcelain-lined or aluminum kettle. To each quart of rind use one teaspoon salt, and water to nearly cover. Boil until tender enough to pierce with a silver fork, or leave in fireless cooker over night. Pour into a colander to drain, dry a few pieces at a time by pressing gently in a crash towel. Make a syrup allowing one quart best cider vinegar to three pounds sugar. Make two small cheese-cloth bags, put into each one teaspoon Larkin Cloves and two tablespoons Larkin Cinnamon, drop these into the syrup and let it boil up, then skim. Put in the melon rind and cook fifteen minutes. Fill sterilized jars with the rind, cover with the boiling syrup, place spice bag on top and seal tight.

MISS CARRIE E. PUGH, BROWNELL, KANS.

Hot Minnesota Pickle

Take twenty-four large tomatoes, two red peppers, two green peppers, four large onions, three heads celery, two cups Larkin Vinegar, one tablespoon salt, three-fourths cup granulated sugar, one teaspoon Larkin Cinnamon. Put tomatoes, onions, celery and peppers through Larkin Food-Chopper using coarse cutter. Add the vinegar, sugar and spice and boil for one hour. Very good with cold meat.

MRS. J. MARASEK, MINNEAPOLIS, MINN.

Uncooked Tomato Pickles

Chop fine one-half peck ripe tomatoes, three heads celery and two red peppers with the seeds removed; add one cup brown sugar, one-half cup salt, one tablespoon Larkin Black Pepper, one teaspoon each ground mace, cloves and cinnamon, two-thirds cup black and white mustard seed mixed, one cup grated horseradish and one quart vinegar. Mix all well together. Put up in jars or bottles. Keep one month before using.

ELIZABETH MARONEY, MELROSE, MASS.

Chili Sauce

Twenty-four red tomatoes, six onions, one and one-half cups sugar, one quart vinegar, one tablespoon each Larkin Salt, Ginger, Cinnamon and Ground Cloves, one green pepper, a little pinch of Larkin Cayenne Pepper and Larkin Mustard. Chop up tomatoes and put green peppers and onions through Larkin Food-Chopper, add rest of ingredients and boil slowly for three or four hours. Put in an air-tight can. Fine with meat.

KATHRYN BUCHANAN, JANESVILLE, WIS.

Bordeaux Sauce

Four quarts cabbage, two quarts green tomatoes, six large onions, two ounces white mustard seed, one-half ounce celery seed, one-half ounce tumeric, three red peppers, two pounds granulated sugar, eight tablespoons salt, two quarts vinegar. Put cabbage, tomatoes and onions through food-chopper; add all the ingredients and boil for thirty minutes. Seal while hot. This makes five quarts.

MISS MARGARET CREIGHTON, LONACONING, MD.

Pepper Relish

Put twelve green tomatoes, four red bell-peppers and two onions through Larkin Food-Chopper, using coarse cutter. Add two-thirds cup sugar, two teaspoons Larkin Salt and two cups vinegar. Mix well and bottle without cooking.

MRS. GEORGE W. QUINT, GRAY, MAINE.

Cherry Olives

Fill a quart jar with nice plump cherries, put one tablespoon Larkin Salt on top and fill jar with white-wine vinegar and seal up. Do not remove the stones. These are ready for use in a few days. This recipe is worth trying.

MRS. D. M. NEWLAN, HOOPESTON, ILL.

Sweet Pickled Cherries

Stone and cover any amount of cherries with vinegar. Let stand all night. In the morning drain off vinegar, put cherries into stone jar and add one pound sugar to every pound of cherries. Let stand nine days stirring three to four times daily. On the ninth day bottle and seal.

MRS. R. V. BUCKAGE, VINCENTOWN, N. J.

Sweet Pickled Peaches

Put two pounds Larkin Brown Sugar, one ounce stick cinnamon and one pint Larkin Vinegar into a preserving kettle. Cook twenty minutes; thinly peel one-half peck peaches and stick each peach with several cloves. Put into the syrup and cook until soft. Seal while hot.

MRS. W. MARSHALL, CHICAGO, ILL.

Corn Salad

Eighteen ears corn, one head cabbage, four onions, three peppers, one and one-half teaspoons ground pepper, one and one-fourth pounds brown sugar, one-fourth cup mustard, one-fourth cup salt, two quarts good vinegar. Chop corn, cabbage, onions and peppers fine, add the other ingredients and cook for fifteen minutes after bringing to the boiling point. This recipe makes about five and one-half quarts. Seal while hot.

MRS. CHRIS. CHRISTENSEN, GARNER, IOWA.

Mixed Pickles

One-half gallon cabbage, one-half gallon cucumbers, one-half gallon green beans, one-half gallon small onions, four green peppers and two red peppers. Use celery seed, horseradish and Larkin Spices to taste. Cook onions and beans tender first, then add cucumbers, cabbage, and tomatoes; mix all together, cover with vinegar, put on the stove, bring to a boil and seal.

MRS. J. M. JINKENS, MEMPHIS, MO.

Canned Cucumbers

Wash cucumbers, pack in fruit jars, cover with cold vinegar; add one tablespoon salt to each two-quart jar, put rubber on and seal tight.

MRS. A. S. LEACH, BROOKLAND, ARK.

Ripe Cucumber Pickles

Cut cucumbers in halves lengthwise. Cover with alum water, allowing two teaspoons powdered alum to each quart of water. Heat gradually to boiling point; then let stand on back of range two hours. Remove from alum water and chill in ice-water. Make syrup by boiling five minutes two pounds sugar, one pint vinegar with two tablespoons each whole cloves and stick cinnamon tied in a piece of muslin. Add cucumbers and cook ten minutes. Remove cucumbers to a stone jar and pour in the syrup. Scald syrup three successive mornings and return to cucumbers.

Mrs. James A. Sipes, Detroit, Mich.

Spiced Cucumber Pickles

To one gallon Larkin Vinegar add one cup each mustard, black pepper, salt and sugar. Put into a jar and mix well. Wash the cucumbers and wipe dry. Place in the vinegar. This is enough for two gallons of cucumbers. They are fine.

Mrs. Ira Carpenter, Algiers, Ind.

Olive Oil Pickles

Cover four quarts sliced cucumbers with boiling hot water and when cold drain and cover with a weak brine. Let stand over night. In the morning drain. Then add one-half teaspoon each of cloves, allspice and celery seed, two teaspoons cinnamon, one-half cup Larkin Olive Oil, one-half cup sugar, one-half cup mustard seed, one dozen onions and cold vinegar enough to cover thoroughly. Mix well and can.

Mrs. Chris. Christensen, Garner, Iowa.

Uncooked Cucumber Relish

Pare six large fresh cucumbers and chop fine, add one tablespoon salt, drain cucumbers in a colander one hour, add three small onions chopped fine, one teaspoon Larkin White Pepper, one pint white-wine vinegar; stir all well together, put into glass jars or bottles, seal air-tight and let stand one month before using.

C. Elizabeth Davidson, Melrose, Mass.

Cucumber Mustard Pickles

Put into a one-quart fruit jar, four tablespoons sugar, two tablespoons each salt and ground mustard (dry). Wash cucumbers and pack as many as possible into jar. Cucumbers should not be more than four inches long. Then fill up jar with cold vinegar. Screw up air-tight. After six weeks they are ready for the table and are delicious. These will keep several years if kept in a cool place.

Mrs. Geo. Sargent, Brainerd, Minn.

Mustard Pickles

One gallon cucumbers, one gallon green tomatoes, one-half gallon onions, one-half gallon cabbage. Cut each separately in small pieces. Add one-half pint salt to one gallon water; soak over night. Drain and add the following: Three quarts Larkin Vinegar, one quart sugar, four tablespoons dry Larkin Mustard, one and one-half tablespoons tumeric, one tablespoon Larkin Cinnamon moistened with a little vinegar. Cook until tender, will keep without sealing.

MRS. JOHN DREITH, LINCOLN, NEBR.

Old Virginia Chow-Chow

Chop fine eight quarts green tomatoes, three small heads cabbage, six large onions, six ripe peppers, six green peppers. Sprinkle with salt, and let stand twenty-four hours; drain thoroughly, add three quarts vinegar, one and one-half pounds brown sugar. Boil all together one hour, then add: Eight quarts ripe tomatoes, three heads finely chopped celery, one pint horseradish, boil another fifteen minutes after which add: One tablespoon each of cloves and mustard, two tablespoons each white mustard seed, allspice and ginger. Mix all together thoroughly, put up in jars and seal. Use Larkin spices, sugar and vinegar.

LEONORA PAGE, AMHERST, MASS.

Beet Relish

Chop one quart cooked beets and one quart raw cabbage, add one cup grated horseradish, one cup granulated sugar, one tablespoon Larkin Salt, one-half teaspoon Larkin Black Pepper. Add only enough vinegar to moisten.

MRS. ELIZA GILLIS, STANHOPE, N. J.

To Can Fruit

The important points in canning are to have the fruit in good condition, the syrup clear, rightly proportioned and boiling hot, the jars hot before putting in the fruit and then filled to overflowing. Keep jars in hot water until needed to fill, stand them in a pan on a folded cloth with a little hot water in the pan. A wide-mouthed funnel is a great aid when doing the work. Have the covers for the jars in another dish of hot water; dip the rubbers as you place them on the jars.

To can small fruits it is better to put the fruit into jars, then pour over the hot syrup and lay on the covers but do not screw down. Put some slats of wood into a wash-boiler so that the jars will stand steady, stand the jars upon them and pour enough warm water into the wash-boiler to come about half way up. Let the water boil five minutes, then take out the jars and screw tight. Always open fruit some time before using; the flavor will be much improved by so doing.

Amount of Sugar

One pound of sugar to one pint of water is a good general rule to follow.

To Can Pears

Allow one-fourth pound of sugar to one pint of water.

To Can Peaches

Allow one-half pound of sugar to one pint of water.

To Can Vegetables

The success of canning vegetables depends chiefly on absolute cleanliness. The jars must have glass or metal covers; do not use those with porcelain lining. All vegetables must be freshly gathered.

Larkin Kitchen.

To Can Peas, Lima or Shell Beans

Fill clean jars with freshly-picked peas, fill each jar with water that has been boiled and cooled, adjust rubbers, lay on covers (do not screw), arrange them in a wash-boiler as directed for fruit and boil continuously for two and one-half hours; lift each jar and screw tight without removing the cover. This rule will answer for lima and other shell beans.

LARKIN KITCHEN.

To Can Corn

Shave corn from the cob, fill jars and press down with a wooden spoon. Be quite sure the jar is full. Seal and stand in Larkin Steam Cooker No. 140. Steam for three hours. If you have no Steam Cooker, place a rack in wash-boiler and surround with cold water. If the corn shrinks and you want to fill up the jars do so quickly, screw down and steam a few minutes longer. Corn canned in this way will keep indefinitely if instructions are observed.

MRS. C. CRANDALL, BUFFALO, N. Y.

Canned Snap Beans

To twelve pints string beans, add one pint salt with water enough to cover beans. Boil until half done. Put into glass jars and cover with brine in which beans have been cooked. Seal while hot.

MRS. JOHN H. DENKER, LAKEFIELD, MINN.

To Can Tomatoes

Put tomatoes into a wire basket or colander, plunge them into boiling water for just a moment, remove skins, cut them in half and press out seeds. Put tomatoes into a clean kettle, boil for about thirty minutes, stirring frequently. If there is much liquid boil a little longer. Then follow instructions given for canning fruit.

LARKIN KITCHEN.

Jellies are made of cooked fruit juice and sugar, in nearly all cases the proportions being equal. Where failures occur, they may usually be traced to the use of too ripe fruit.

To Prepare Glasses for Jelly

Wash glasses and put into a kettle of cold water; place on range and heat water gradually to boiling point. Remove glasses and drain. Place glasses while filling on a cloth wrung out of hot water.

To Cover Jelly Glasses

Melt paraffin and cover jelly, then adjust cover.

To Make a Jelly Bag

Fold two opposite corners of a piece of wool-and-cotton flannel about three-fourths yard square. Sew up in form of a cornucopia, rounding at the top. Fell the seam to make more secure. Bind the top with tape, and furnish with two or three heavy loops by which it may be hung.

LARKIN KITCHEN.

Apple Jelly

Take twelve good-sized apples, wipe with a clean cloth and cut in quarters. Cover with two quarts cold water. Leave over night. In the morning stew until the liquid is about half cooked away. Then add the juice of two lemons. Boil ten minutes. Allow the juice to drip through double cheese-cloth. Measure the juice, put an equal quantity of sugar in a granite dish in the oven to warm. Stir occasionally. When the juice begins to jelly round the edge of the pan, add the sugar, boil five minutes, skim and pour into heated jelly glasses. Cover and keep in a cold dry place.

MRS. W. E. BROOKS, LOS MOLINOS, CAL.

Preserved Cherries

To a full pint of stoned cherries take one and one-fourth cups sugar. Boil twenty minutes and turn out into a crock to cool. When cold, put into jars. Boil only one quart of fruit at a time.

MISS FLORENCE ADRIAN, EDINBURG, ILL.

Preserved Figs

Put ripe figs into a pan. Strew Larkin Soda thickly over the figs, cover with boiling water and stand aside until cool. Make a syrup with one pound sugar and one quart water. When the figs are cool take from soda-water and cook in syrup until clear. Put into jars and seal.

MRS. JAMES R. WILKERSON, WALDO, FLA.

Strawberry Preserves (Sun-cooked)

Weigh the strawberries, take as much sugar as fruit, put on stove, bring to a boil, have large meat platters ready to put fruit on and stand in the sun all day. The sun draws out the water and the berries retain their full size. If the sun should not shine all day, put out the fruit a second day, then put into glass jars. One trial will convince any cook how delicious and easy these preserves are. Cherries can be cooked likewise. If it is not possible to put the fruit outside in the sun, cook for five minutes and then seal.

MRS. FRANK H. GODAR, LOUISVILLE, KY.

Pineapple and Strawberry Preserve

To one cup grated pineapple allow two cups strawberries and three cups sugar. Boil for twenty minutes, fill jelly glasses; seal when cold.

MRS. F. L. MYER, EAST ST. LOUIS, ILL.

Rhubarb Conserve

Take six pounds rhubarb cut in small pieces, one pound sun-dried figs cut in strips or put through food-chopper, one-half pound English walnuts and five pounds sugar. Put the sugar over rhubarb, leave over night; in the morning cook until thick, then add figs. Cook another thirty minutes, add walnuts, coarsely chopped, and remove from fire. Put into jelly glasses and, when cold, cover with paraffin. Store in a cool, dark place. This is delicious.

MRS. F. A. SMITH, SALAMANCA, N. Y.

Grape Conserve

Take ten pounds ripe grapes, separate skins from pulp, cook pulp separately (just enough to separate seeds), put through colander; then cook the pulp, skins and ten pounds of Larkin Granulated Sugar together for twenty minutes. Grate the rind from four or five oranges, peel off the white pith, add the pulp and one pound of cut-up Larkin Seeded Raisins to the grapes, cook twenty minutes, then seal tight. Delicious.

MISS JEAN HAUSER, WILKES BARRE, PA.

Plum Conserve

Use this rule for any fruit. Stew two and one-half quarts plums with one and one-half cups water until very soft. Strain through a colander, mash with a wooden spoon. Add as much granulated sugar as you have pulp. Put through food-chopper two oranges, one small lemon, one pound seeded raisins, one-half pound walnut meats and one-half pound sun-dried figs. Use rind of oranges and lemon as well as pulp. Cook all together fifteen minutes, being careful not to burn. This is delicious for sandwiches or to serve with Chicken or Turkey.

MRS. R. DUBUC, BERLIN, N. H.

Red Currant Conserve

Pick four pounds of red currants from the stems. Wash and put them into a preserving kettle with one pound seeded raisins cut in halves, three pounds sugar and four lemons. Peel the lemons very thin, remove the white pith and seeds and cut in thin slices. Boil to a thick jam. If you like spice, add one teaspoon Larkin Cinnamon and one-half teaspoon Larkin Cloves.

CLARA E. COOPER, ASHLAND, MASS.

Orange Marmalade

Shred one thin-skinned orange and one thin-skinned lemon with a paring knife. Put into a New Idea Kettle (No. 210). To each measure of shredded fruit take three of water, cover and set aside for twenty-four hours. Put on fire and boil fifteen minutes. Set aside for another twenty-four hours. Measure contents in kettle. To every seven cups of pulp use eight cups of Larkin Granulated Sugar (buy sugar in a twenty-five pound bag). Boil until it jells which will be in about twenty minutes, pour into jelly glasses, cover with paraffin. One orange and one lemon with quantities given will make seven glasses of marmalade at a cost of less than three cents a glass.

MRS. EDWARD HIEBEL, HOLYOKE, MASS.

Grapefruit Marmalade

Slice very thin, one orange, one lemon and one grapefruit, leaving out the bitter center of grapefruit. Add eight cups water and set aside twenty-four hours. Boil twenty minutes and set aside another twenty-four hours. Measure and add an equal quantity of sugar and boil until it jells. This will make one dozen glasses. For a delicious sherbet, add one pint of good lemonade to two glasses of marmalade. Freeze.

MRS. CHARLES WALKER SCHLAGEL, DES PLAINES, ILL.

Carrot Marmalade

Scald and rub the skin from a number of carrots. Then put the carrots through the food-chopper. To each pint of the pulp add the juice and grated rind of one lemon. Put into a sauce-pan. For each quart pour over the mixture three and one-half cups Larkin Granulated Sugar and let it stand all night. In the morning boil until it is clear and appears sufficiently cooked. Put into jelly glasses. This is a particularly delicious marmalade and so economical that almost anyone may enjoy it.

MISS CHARLOTTE BIRD, ANN ARBOR, MICH.

Rhubarb Jam

Wash and cut up without removing the skin, seven pounds rhubarb. Put into the kettle with five pounds sugar, one pound seeded raisins and two oranges thinly sliced. Cook until very thick taking care not to let it burn. Put into glasses and seal.

MRS. M. STOTT, DORMANSVILLE, N. Y.

Pear Chips

Eight pounds pears, six pounds Larkin Sugar, three lemons, one quart cold water, one-eighth pound ginger root. Cut the pears fine, grate the lemons and squeeze out the juice. Now add the sugar, water and ginger root; cook slowly for three hours.

MRS. G. E. LARRABEE, BINGHAMTON, N. Y.

Quince Honey

Pare and grate five large quinces. To one pint boiling water add five pounds sugar. Stir over fire until sugar is dissolved, add quince and cook fifteen or twenty minutes. Turn into glasses. When cold it should be about the color and consistency of honey.

MRS. S. W. WARD, FALLSTON, MD.

Coffee Cleared with Egg

For six cups of boiled coffee mix three-fourths cup ground coffee, one-third of the white of an egg and one-half cup cold water in the coffee-pot. Pour over this one quart boiling water, stir thoroughly. Boil three minutes. Stir again and stand on back of stove, where it will not boil, for ten minutes. Be careful to see that the coffee spout is free from grounds before pouring. Never boil coffee furiously or the true flavor will be lost.

LARKIN KITCHEN.

Coffee without Egg

Allow two tablespoons of coffee for each cup. Scald the coffee-pot. Pour boiling water on the coffee and boil five minutes. Set it back where it will keep hot, but not boil. Add a little cold water; pour out a little coffee and pour back again, to clear the spout. Or the coffee and cold water may be put together in the pot over night and brought to the boiling point in the morning. To use a Larkin Percolator is much the best and easiest method.

LARKIN KITCHEN.

Tea

Scald the teapot and use two teaspoons of tea to each pint of boiling water; stir the tea and it is ready to serve. Never use a metal pot for tea, as the tannic acid acts on the metal, making the tea unwholesome.

LARKIN KITCHEN.

Cocoa

Scald three cups milk in a Larkin Double-Boiler. Mix thoroughly three tablespoons Larkin Cocoa with two tablespoons sugar, a few grains of salt and add, while stirring constantly, one cup boiling water. Boil three minutes and pour into the hot milk. Beat several minutes with a wire whisk or egg-beater. This is called milling and will prevent a scum from rising. Flavor with one-half teaspoon vanilla extract. Use whipped cream or a marshmallow in each cup.

ZULA BREEDEN, HASKELL, OKLA.

Chocolate

Two ounces Larkin Unsweetened Chocolate, four tablespoons sugar, one cup boiling water, few grains of salt, three cups milk. Scald milk. Melt chocolate in small sauce-pan placed over hot water, add sugar, salt and boiling water gradually, when smooth, place on range and boil one minute; add to scalded milk, and serve in chocolate cups with whipped cream. One and one-half ounces sweet chocolate may be substituted for the unsweetened chocolate. Being sweetened, less sugar is required.

LARKIN KITCHEN.

Grape Juice

Wash and stem grapes (Concords preferred). Measure, and to every four quarts grapes before cooking, add one quart cold water. Boil until soft. Remove from fire and when cool enough to handle, strain through a coarse cloth twice to extract juice. Measure again and to each quart of juice add one cup of Larkin Granulated Sugar. Place on fire and boil ten minutes. Remove and bottle at once. Seal air-tight with Larkin Paraffin Wax.

MRS. FLORENCE HALL, NATICK, MASS.

Shrub

Almost any small fruits may be used for this, but raspberries are particularly good. Berries that are not nice enough for the table or those that are gathered damp may be used for this syrup. Allow the berries to ferment, then strain and use one cup of sugar to one quart of juice. Boil fifteen minutes, if not sufficiently acid, add a little vinegar. Use two teaspoons to a glass of water.

MRS. J. S. MILLS, SOUTH ASHBURNHAM, MASS.

Fruit Juice and Syrup

Secure perfectly ripe fruit, cook with about one-fourth as much water as you have fruit. Press out the juice and strain as if for jelly. Sweeten to taste and boil for twenty minutes in a preserving kettle. If for syrup, use equal amounts of sugar and juice. Have clean sterilized bottles standing in a pan of boiling water and corks that will fit completely down inside bottle mouths and one cup of melted Larkin Paraffin Wax. Fill each bottle with the boiling juice to within one and one-half inches of the top. Press down a heated cork until it touches the juice and fill the remaining space above the cork with melted paraffin, adding more as it hardens until a complete cap is formed around the top of mouth. This will keep for any length of time if stored in a cool, dark place.

ELIZABETH MARONEY, MELROSE, MASS.

Lemon Syrup or Fresh Lemonade

Boil one cup sugar and two cups water twelve minutes, add one-third cup lemon juice to syrup. Dilute with ice-water as needed. Good for picnics. For fresh lemonade put one teaspoon sugar into a glass; add the juice of one-half lemon. Stir until sugar is melted. Fill glass with cold water and it is ready to serve.

LARKIN KITCHEN.

Fruit Punch

Make one quart strong tea (using Larkin Mixed or Ceylon Tea) add sugar to hot tea. Make one-half gallon lemonade with six lemons and four oranges. The oranges may be cut in small pieces; add one can Larkin Pineapple cut in small pieces, one bottle Maraschino cherries, one-half pound Malaga grapes with seeds removed; sweeten to taste. This makes about one and one-half gallons. Any fruit juice on hand may be used with this. Serve very cold.

MRS. V. W. CASTEN, SUFFOLK, VA.

Club-of-Ten Punch

Pour one pint of hot water over the grated rind of one lemon and one pound of sugar. Boil five minutes. Strain, and while still hot, slice into it two medium-sized bananas and three large peaches (canned peaches may be used and put in when cold). Add a cup of grated pineapple (either fresh or canned), one pint of canned cherries, the juice of seven lemons and two oranges. Put a large block of ice in the center of the punch-bowl, add two quarts of water and let stand two hours in a cool place. At the last moment add a few fine strawberries. This will serve twenty-five people.

NAME NOT GIVEN.

Ice-Cream Candy

Boil two cups sugar with one-half cup water, one tablespoon vinegar, one tablespoon butter. Do not stir the mixture. Boil until crisp when tried in cold water; when cooked add one-half teaspoon vanilla extract. When cool pull until white, the longer you pull the better the candy.

MISS EVELYN WHITNEY, ATTLEBORO, MASS.

Chocolate Cream Candy

Two cups sugar, two-thirds cup milk, one tablespoon butter, two squares chocolate (four tablespoons cocoa may be used instead of chocolate), one teaspoon vanilla. Put butter into granite sauce-pan; when melted add sugar and milk. Heat to boiling point; then add chocolate and stir constantly until chocolate is melted. Boil until a little dropped into cold water will form a soft ball. Remove from fire, add vanilla, cool and beat until creamy and mixture begins to sugar slightly around edge of sauce-pan. Pour at once into a buttered pan, cool slightly, and mark in squares. One-half cup nuts or raisins may be added.

MRS. R. ROMMEL, ELIZABETH, N. J.

Cocoanut Bars

To one pound or two and one-half cups powdered sugar, use the juice of one lemon, white of one egg, and make into a smooth ball. Roll into a sheet one-half inch thick, sprinkle thickly with Larkin Shredded Cocoanut; put one-half upon the other and cut into bars.

MRS. HAEFNER, PHILADELPHIA, PA.

Nut Loaf Candy

Two pounds granulated sugar, one and one-half cups Larkin Corn Syrup, one-half cup boiling water, one-half pound English walnut meats, whites of two eggs beaten light. Boil the sugar, water and syrup until it hardens when dropped into cold water. Pour slowly over the whites of the eggs. Stir in one-fourth teaspoon Larkin Vanilla Flavoring Extract and the nuts; beat until light. Then pour out and cut into squares.

MISS REBA PETERS, OTTERBEIN, IND.

Candy Baskets

Take one cup sugar, one-half cup water, a pinch of cream of tartar and stir together. Put on stove and boil (do not stir after it is on the stove) until it cracks when dropped into cold water. When it is almost done it becomes very bubbly. Pour it out on a buttered slab and gradually work it into a ball or lump, by folding the edges into the center. When cool enough to handle, add one-fourth teaspoon Larkin Culinary Paste Color moistened with one-half teaspoon Larkin Flavoring Extract. Then pull and form into baskets making each a different shape. Butter the hands occasionally while pulling. These quantities will make three small baskets. It is well to keep in mind that these extracts and colors go together: When wintergreen extract is used, color with red culinary paste. When lemon use yellow; when spearmint use green; when nutmeg, green and red mixed, using twice as much green as red—you will then have gray; when orange use red and yellow; when cinnamon use heliotrope; sassafras use very little yellow; peppermint use no color. If you do not care to make the baskets the recipe is equally good for candies. They may be cut in strips or formed into small balls. For a children's party the baskets make a delightful decoration or gift especially as they are good to eat as well as to look at.

Mrs. Edward H. Schell, Harrisburg, Pa.

Fruit Candy

This is candy you can let the children make. Wash one cup each Larkin Figs, Dates and Prunes; add one cup seeded raisins and walnut meats. Put all through the food-chopper. Mix thoroughly and it is ready to use. Form into small balls, dip in melted chocolate and place on waxed paper to dry. Cherries, nuts, pieces of candied pineapple may all be used for the center; if fillings are used you may then call them Surprise Balls, others may be dipped in fondant used for making candy baskets. This fruit is also delicious as a sandwich filling.

Cecelia Hahn, Wabash, Ind.

Cream Caramels

One-half cake or four ounces Larkin Unsweetened Chocolate, one pound Larkin Powdered Sugar, one scant cup milk, one-half cup butter. Boil these together from five to eight minutes or until the mixture scrapes off white from the side of the pan. Take from fire, add one teaspoon vanilla and beat hard until it thickens, pour into well-greased pan and when nearly cold cut in squares.

Mrs. Henry M. Buettner, Baltimore, Md.

Fondant

Two and one-half pounds sugar, one and one-half cups boiling water, one-fourth teaspoon cream of tartar. Stir ingredients together, heat slowly to boiling point; then boil without stirring until a soft ball will form when dropped into a little cold water. Pour fondant into a shallow pan, flavor with any Larkin Flavoring Extract, let stand a few minutes to cool but not long enough to become hard around the edge; stir with a wooden paddle until white and creamy. It will quickly change from this consistency and begin to lump, when it should be kneaded with the hands until perfectly smooth.

Put into a bowl, cover with oiled paper and stand aside for twenty-four hours if possible. It will then be found easier to use. Always make fondant on a clear, dry day. Cream Nut Bars, Cream Mints and various candies may all be made with this fondant.

Shirley M. Shaffer, Oil City, Pa.

Cocoanut Fudge

Two cups sugar, two-thirds cup milk, put into a sauce-pan and cook over moderate fire until a little dropped into cold water will form a soft ball. Remove from fire, add two tablespoons butter, cool and add one teaspoon vanilla extract, one-half cup shredded cocoanut and one-half cup chopped walnuts. Beat all together until the mixture begins to thicken, then spread upon buttered tin to thickness of one-half inch. Cut into squares.

Mrs. George W. Quint, Gray, Maine.

Peanut Butter Fudge

Cook together two cups granulated sugar, two tablespoons peanut butter and one-half cup milk until it forms a soft ball when dropped into cold water. Add one-half teaspoon Larkin Vanilla Flavoring Extract, cool and beat until creamy. Pour onto a buttered pie-plate and when nearly cold cut in small squares.

Mrs. G. C. Caslan, Washington, D. C.

Pinoche or Divinity

Take two pounds or four cups Larkin Brown Sugar, one cup milk, one-half cup butter, one cup walnuts chopped fine (or any other nuts), one-half teaspoon salt. Boil the sugar, milk, butter and salt until it forms a soft ball in cold water. Remove from stove, add one teaspoon vanilla, cool, add the nuts and beat until nearly hard. Pour into buttered pans, mark off in squares when cold. For divinity pour the boiling syrup over the stiffly-beaten whites of two eggs, add nuts and vanilla and beat until mixture will stand alone.

Miss A. Rommel, Elizabeth, N. J.

Sultana Caramels

Two cups Larkin Sugar, one-half cup milk, one-fourth cup molasses, one-half cup butter, two squares Larkin Chocolate, one teaspoon vanilla, one-half cup English walnut or hickory nut meats cut in pieces, two tablespoons Sultana raisins. Put butter and chocolate into a sauce-pan; when melted, add sugar, milk and molasses. Heat to boiling point, and boil seven minutes longer. Remove from fire, beat until creamy, add nuts, raisins and vanilla; pour at once into a buttered tin. Cool slightly and mark in squares.

Mrs. Frank L. Hinds, Northampton, Mass.

Larkin Mints

Put one cup cold water into a sauce-pan, add four cups granulated sugar and one tablespoon butter. Boil without stirring until it forms a soft ball when dropped into cold water. Take from fire and cool slightly; add one-half teaspoon each of peppermint and apple-green culinary paste. Beat until creamy. Drop by teaspoonfuls on waxed paper. Make the same quantity again and color pink, flavor with Larkin Wintergreen. These mints are delicious to serve after a heavy meal or with afternoon tea.

Mrs. John McKee, Moriah Center, N. Y.

Marshmallows

Take two cups granulated sugar, add six tablespoons water, stir over a moderate fire until it boils, then boil without stirring until a little dropped into cold water will form a soft ball. Have ready two tablespoons Larkin Gelatine soaked in six tablespoons cold water about ten minutes. Pour into the candy and stir and beat until thick. Flavor with Larkin Vanilla or Orange Flavoring Extract; pour into a dish well powdered with pulverized sugar and spread to the thickness of one inch, sprinkle with the powdered sugar and put in cool place over night. Then cut into squares with knife that has been dipped in boiling water, dip edges in the sugar and pack in boxes lined with Larkin Waxed Paper.

Miss Annie E. Graybill, Buchanan, Va.

Children's Raisin Candy

One cup powdered sugar, two tablespoons Larkin Cocoa, two tablespoons melted butter and enough boiling water to mix stiff. Flavor with one-half teaspoon vanilla. Take a little of the mixture on the end of a teaspoon and form into a ball, taking two raisins to each ball and press together until nearly flat. If white candy is preferred leave out cocoa.

Mrs. P. E. Monroe, South Weymouth, Mass.

Vinegar Taffy

Two cups granulated sugar, one-half cup hot water, two tablespoons butter. Place on fire, when it comes to a boil add five tablespoons acid vinegar. Boil until brittle when tested in cold water. Pour into buttered pan until cool enough to pull.

MRS. HENRY DAVIS, NEW DECATUR, ALA.

Larkin Cocoa Caramels

One cup Larkin Molasses or Corn Syrup, one cup brown sugar, one cup milk, three tablespoons butter, one-half cup cocoa, one teaspoon vanilla. Boil sugar, molasses, milk and cocoa until it forms a hard ball in cold water. Add butter and vanilla when nearly done. Cut when cool.

MRS. HENRY M. BUETTNER, BALTIMORE, MD.

Ham Sandwich Filling

One cup or one-half pound chopped ham, enough good vinegar to moisten well, one tablespoon Larkin Peanut Butter, a few drops of Larkin Celery Flavoring Extract, pepper and salt to taste. Mix well and you will have the best ham sandwich you ever ate.

MRS. W. L. UMBARGER, KONNAROCK, VA.

Cheese Olive Sandwiches

One-fourth can Larkin Pimentos, one ten-cent cream cheese (little snappy), twelve soda crackers, six Larkin Olives, one medium-sized onion. Put all these through a Larkin Food-Chopper, mix with Larkin Salad Dressing. Season with pepper and salt, spread on thin slices of bread with a lettuce leaf between.

MRS. D. B. SMITH, FOSTORIA, OHIO.

Pimento Cheese Sandwiches

One small can Larkin Pimentos, one pound Larkin Cream Cheese, one very small onion, put all through the meat-chopper. Mix with boiled salad dressing. Spread between thin slices of bread and butter.

MRS. FRED ALLSOPP, PONTIAC, ILL.

Roquefort Cheese Sandwiches

One-half pound Roquefort cheese, one cream cheese, one bottle Larkin Stuffed Olives, one small onion, one head celery, three green peppers, one-half cup butter. Grind all together in Larkin Food-Chopper and serve between crackers or sliced bread. Half these quantities make enough for a large crowd.

MRS. CHARLES KELSEY, ST. JOHNSVILLE, N. Y.

American Cheese Sandwiches

Cream the yolk of a hard-boiled egg with a tablespoon of melted butter, add a little salt, white pepper and mustard and one-quarter pound grated cheese; stir in a scant tablespoon of vinegar and spread between thin slices of bread with a lettuce leaf or cress.

MRS. JOHN CARPER, FRANKLIN, NEBR.

Larkin Sandwiches

Put six hard-boiled eggs and six Larkin Sweet Pickles through Larkin Food-Chopper. Mix thoroughly, add two tablespoons Larkin Peanut Butter, salt and pepper to suit taste. Then add Larkin Prepared Mustard and a little vinegar to the consistency of spreading.

MISS MAUDE BRILES, FAIRMOUNT, IND.

Scrambled-Egg Sandwiches

Chip left-over ham and one small onion in small pieces, then add it to one well-beaten egg and fry in butter. Salt and pepper to taste. This makes a fine sandwich.

MRS. WM. R. TREON, TURBOTVILLE, PA.

Pork and Bean Sandwiches

Cut thin slices from a loaf of brown bread, butter and put crisp lettuce leaves with a teaspoon of Mayonnaise dressing on one slice. On the other spread a layer of pork and beans which have been mashed until smooth. Put slices together and wrap each sandwich separately in waxed paper. Delicious for school or picnic lunches.

MRS. PEARL M. HACKER, COUNCIL BLUFFS, IOWA.

Peanut Sandwich Filling

Mix Larkin Peanut Butter with a small amount of Larkin Prepared Mustard, add a little cream or Larkin Evaporated Milk. The proportions may vary to suit the taste. Spread on thinly-sliced graham bread, cut cross-wise and serve on lettuce leaves or decorate with parsley or cress.

MRS. ERIC H. LINDQUIST, STROMSBURG, NEBR.

Sweet Peanut Sandwiches

One-half cup grated maple sugar, one-fourth cup finely-chopped peanuts, one tablespoon rich sweet milk. Mix well and spread between thin slices of graham or plain bread.

MRS. A. B. GRACIA, NEW BEDFORD, MASS.

Fruit Sandwiches

One pound each Larkin Dates and English walnuts, three tablespoons sweet cream. Put both dates and nuts through meat-chopper using the fine knife. Mix until smooth adding a tablespoon of cream as needed. Makes about four dozen sandwiches and filling will keep a long time in cool weather. Used with whole-wheat bread makes delicious sandwiches.

MRS. CLIFF HARRIS, MAXWELL, ILL.

Sardine Sandwiches

Take one small can Larkin Sardines, the juice of a small lemon and one tablespoon salad dressing. Mix in a bowl with a fork; spread on bread or Larkin Soda Crackers. Fine for outings or company.

MRS. N. T. WALSH, BROOKLYN, N. Y.

Tomato and Onion Sandwiches

Cut very firm tomatoes into slices as thin as possible without breaking and wafer-like slices of very white onions. Season with salt and Larkin Cayenne Pepper, add a dash of Larkin Salad Dressing. Put between crisp Larkin Saltines.

CATHERINE NEHAN, GENESEO, N. Y.

Fig Filling for Sandwiches

Chop fine six preserved figs and one-half cup walnuts and mix with enough Larkin Raspberry Jam to spread well. Butter thin slices of Larkin Brown Bread, spread with the filling and cut the slices in quarters.

FLORENCE C. THAYER, STONEHAM, MASS.

INDEX

INDEX

INDEX

INDEX

INDEX

Good Results in Cooking

Good recipes produce good results *only* when good materials are used.

Good materials are not necessarily those that cost the most, for often you will pay the highest price for materials of inferior grade.

Many good recipes are often condemned because of the use of poor materials. Therefore be sure that the materials you use are good quality, that the flavoring extracts or spices are full strength and that the utensils used are the proper ones.

Use Larkin Products

You will have better results, greater satisfaction and at the same time effect a noteworthy saving if you always use Larkin Products.

Pure Foods

Larkin Pure Foods are of the highest quality, always fresh, full-weight, clean and wholesome.

Our Flavoring Extracts are the highest concentrations, our Pure Ground Spices the fullest strength. Our Macaroni, Egg Noodles, Corn Starch, Tapioca, Shredded Cocoanut, Gelatine and Chocolate are articles of exceptional merit with which delicious dishes can be prepared.

Quality in Baking Powder is of vital importance. On it depends success or failure in baking. Larkin Baking Powder is made of the purest materials. It combines the highest baking efficiency with excellent keeping properties and may always be depended on to give uniform results. Always use Larkin Baking Powder.

Larkin Teas are of superior quality. They offer the opportunity to secure delicious tea at a great saving.

All the other Larkin Pure Foods are of the same high quality as those here mentioned. It is wise economy to keep your pantry well stocked with these excellent Products.

Kitchen Cutlery

Every capable housewife knows how essential it is to have in her kitchen well-made cutting implements with keen and lasting edges. Larkin Household Cutlery offers a splendid assortment of high-grade kitchen knives that will give complete and lasting satisfaction.

A Larkin Food-Chopper will add greatly to the efficiency of the kitchen.

You Get Extra Value

Remember, when you buy Larkin Products you get Merchandise-Bonus which gives you double or almost double value for your money.

Before you buy an article at the store, look through your Larkin Catalog—see whether you can buy it as a Larkin Product at Factory-to-Family price or get it *without extra expense* as Larkin Premium Merchandise.

"See First If Larkin Sells It"

Printed in the USA
CPSIA information can be obtained
at www.ICGtesting.com
LVHW091249111223
766160LV00003B/9